"*Listen* is the first and most important word for crafting a personal rule of life. In this helpful resource, you are invited into a spacious place to listen to the still, small voice of God beckoning you into a life of love. From a listening posture, you become more agile to respond to the transformational way of life that Jesus invites, which is far better than the hurried, cluttered, and distracted alternative."

STEPHEN A. MACCHIA, founder and president of Leadership Transformations, director of the Pierce Center at Gordon-Conwell Theological Seminary, and author of sixteen books, including *Crafting a Rule of Life*, *The Discerning Life*, and the bestselling *Becoming a Healthy Church*

"With *The Spacious Path*, Tamara Hill Murphy introduces us to a life-giving rhythm of living. This way invites us to listen deeply to Jesus and respond to his invitations that offer us the peace and rest we need for living a life of love. Her rich work reveals many specific ways that we can feel God's embrace; and even better, how we can always begin again. Tamara is a trusty guide."

LISA COLÓN DELAY, spiritual formation author of *The Wild Land Within* and host of the *Spark My Muse* podcast

"One way to challenge the never-ending demands—all marked URGENT!—that shout at us every day is to embrace Tamara Hill Murphy's wise, grace-soaked counsel to develop a rule for life. The word *rule* may connote yet another crop of to-dos to add to your hectic schedule, but Murphy offers the opposite in *The Spacious Path*. She invites readers into a life of freedom shaped by intentional, reflective choices that help filter out the frantic and make space for the things which matter most."

MICHELLE VAN LOON, author of *Translating Your Past: Finding Meaning in Family Ancestry, Genetic Clues, and Generational Trauma*

"Many people feel overwhelmed by life these days, and for good reason. 'Normal' appears as a distant dot in the rearview mirror. But what if instead of normal, we sought a graced and spacious life? Tamara Hill Murphy invites us into such a life. In *The Spacious Path*, we are reminded that God has provided wide-open spaces for us, and that we can live a life 'earthed in Christ.' Tamara graciously invites us, and then walks with us, on the path toward engaging a rule of life—one that points to Jesus as our firm foundation."

GEM FADLING, cofounder of Unhurried Living, Inc., and author of *Hold That Thought: Sorting Through the Voices in Our Heads*

"Tamara Murphy's invitation to rest on the spacious path is a beautifully written invitation to walk with Jesus in an easy rhythm, pace, and practice that drew me ever closer to the heart of God. The more I read, the more my desire for intimacy with Jesus grew. In this spacious place there is room to hold the paradox that embraces structure and spaciousness, commitment and freedom, contemplation and community. This book welcomes it all."

MARSHA CROCKETT, author of *Sacred Conversation: Exploring the Seven Gifts of Spiritual Direction*

THE SPACIOUS PATH

THE

Practicing the Restful Way of Jesus

SPACIOUS

in a Fragmented World

PATH

TAMARA HILL MURPHY

Foreword by W. David O. Taylor

HERALD
PRESS

Harrisonburg, Virginia

Herald Press
PO Box 866, Harrisonburg, Virginia 22803
www.HeraldPress.com

Study guides are available for many Herald Press titles at www.HeraldPress.com.

THE SPACIOUS PATH
© 2023 by Herald Press, Harrisonburg, Virginia 22803. 800-245-7894.
    All rights reserved.
Library of Congress Control Number: 2023004016
International Standard Book Number: 978-1-5138-1191-8 (paperback);
    978-1-5138-1192-5 (hardcover); 978-1-5138-1193-2 (ebook)
Printed in United States of America

27 26 25 24 23   10 9 8 7 6 5 4 3 2 1

CONTENTS

PART 4:
BLESSING A RULE OF LIFE ON THE SPACIOUS PATH *201*

To Brian, my beloved companion:

*"Love has taught the soul to travel Love's paths,
and the soul has followed them faithfully . . ."*

FOREWORD

As an Enneagram 5 and an INTJ on the Myers-Briggs personality typologies, I love to be maximally productive and minimally inefficient, and I don't take failure well. I take the injunction of Psalm 90:12—that we learn to number our days so that we may attain a heart of wisdom—and I turn it into a campaign to be stupendously prolific in Jesus' name.

Add to this the fact that, as a perpetual late bloomer, I always feel as if I'm playing catch-up with my peers on the professional front. Whatever project I've recently completed never feels good enough. So the only thing to do, in order to feel better about myself, is to get on with the next.

I'm tired all the time. I resist all invitations to slow down. I don't, in fact, make the most of my days but only become anxious about the seeming waste of them. And I can't figure out how to escape the software that's running in my brain that compels me to keep driving harder.

I need help.

I hear Jesus tell the crowds to come to him if they are weary and heavy-laden so that he might give them the rest that they need, and to take up his yoke because it's easy, but I don't think I've ever really believed him. What does a "yoke" even look like?

It looks like a Rule of Life.

But as someone who grew up as a conservative Protestant in a largely Catholic country, when I heard the word "rule," I instinctually heard "dead rituals" and "papist" impositions upon the free spirit of the evangelical at heart.

But I also think that many of us as Protestants today, as I did then, overestimate our capacity to will the right thing. Sheer willpower, in actual point of fact, has an expiration date.

We wish to be free of "religion" so that we can be given over to "relationship," but instead of being truly free, we find ourselves beholden to impossible metrics of religious success and oppressive expectations for spiritual productivity that invisibly but inexorably govern our deepest desires.

We also underestimate the power of liturgies, in the sense of a rhythmed and ordered way of life, to orient our wills, along with our hearts and minds, toward the good by way of our bodies.

What we need, then, is something far more comprehensive than our usual quiet times and pep rallies for Jesus. We need something like a Rule of Life, which might yoke our whole selves to a graced pattern of work and rest, play and prayer, silence and service, fasting and friendship.

But without skilled guides like Tamara Murphy to instruct and inspire us in this new way of being in the world, many of us will likely give up. It's simply too demanding for individuals to embrace on their own.

And this is one of the many gifts that Tamara offers to her readers. She offers herself, not as one who "has arrived," but as one who is continually "on the way." She offers herself as a gentle voice, not a nagging one.

And she offers herself as an honest co-pilgrim, rather than a patronizing one, for she repeatedly acknowledges all the ways that she has failed her own Rule. And in acknowledging such failure, she gives her readers refreshing permission to fail without shame and to try again.

"Always we begin again," Tamara writes, quoting Saint Benedict.

My sincerest hope is that you will find here as much encouragement as I have to try out a Rule of Life and to trust that the spacious, but disciplined, way of Jesus in such a "rule" is the way of deep rest that your body and soul deeply long for.

And if you fail, do take Tamara's advice to heart: be gentle with yourself, as Jesus himself is gentle with you. You can always try again. In fact, that just might be the whole point of the Christian life: that we get to keep trying, and in so doing, to discover that Jesus is right there, *with us*, in the trying.

—W. David O. Taylor
associate professor of theology
and culture at Fuller Theological
Seminary and author of *A Body of
Praise: Understanding the Role of
Our Physical Bodies in Worship*

INTRODUCTION

Thus says the LORD: Stand at the crossroads and look, and ask for the ancient paths, where the good way lies; and walk in it, and find rest for your souls.

—JEREMIAH 6:16 (NRSVUE)

The difference between a path and a road is not only the obvious one. A path is little more than a habit that comes with knowledge of a place. It is a sort of ritual of familiarity. As a form, it is a form of contact with a known landscape. It is not destructive. It is the perfect adaptation, through experience and familiarity, of movement to place; it obeys the natural contours; such obstacles as it meets, it goes around.

—WENDELL BERRY[1]

Just outside Temple, Texas, ten miles from the frenzied traffic of I-35, a quiet Catholic center invites weary retreatants to gather for worship, rest, and meditation. The center sits on seventy-five acres of Texas cedar trees and, in the spring, fields of bluebonnets surrounding several lodges, a couple of stone chapels, and in the middle of it all, an impressive outdoor prayer labyrinth. Modeled after the famous medieval labyrinth gracing the floor of Chartres Cathedral[2] in France, the

Cedarbrake labyrinth embraces its Texas geography, from the native limestone marking the concentric circles of the pathway to the gnarly cedar trees incorporated into the design. Prayerful pilgrims circle the labyrinth, meditating on promises of God or offering petitions for their weary souls, while simultaneously stepping over roots and bending under low branches as they make their way to rest on one of the three stone benches in the center. After silent reflection in the innermost circle of the labyrinth, retreat guests reverse the process, asking God to help them hold on to whatever gift God has given them in prayer as they slowly circle outward, back to the entrance of the path.

During my family's five years in Austin, I was one of those prayerful pilgrims. The first time I'd ever seen or heard of a prayer labyrinth was when I visited the retreat center in the spring of 2013. Eighteen months earlier, we had moved with our four high school-aged children from our hometown in central New York state for my husband's new job at a church in the heart of Texas. After living in one place for forty years, the move felt dramatic and disorienting. We had lost the familiar roadways of home. Literally. We quickly discovered that if homesickness didn't ruin us, then the nerve-wracking maze of Austin's highway system would. It wasn't only the maddening traffic or the confluence of overpasses, underpasses, and service roads that threatened our ability to assimilate to this new place—the geography itself bewildered me.

I'd traveled the roadways of my hometown for so long that my entire sense of direction was formed by upstate New York's rolling hills blanketed in trees, which faithfully transitioned from bare branches to lush green to stunning autumnal colors every year. Until I moved away, I never realized how much I depended on my surroundings to orient me in place and time. On more than one occasion, after the GPS once again failed to offer accurate instructions around Austin, I pulled out to the side of the highway to rail against the cursed concrete of the Texas road system and the flattened, monochromatic landscape that surrounded me. During one of those weeping episodes, I began to panic that I might *never* find my way back home. Although we had been welcomed by the Texas-sized hospitality of our new congregation, it was at the prayer retreat led by our pastor's wife almost two years after we arrived in Austin where I first began to feel grounded in our new state and oriented in our new community.

Silently walking the prayer labyrinth in the quiet retreat center, in the middle of the disorienting season of our family's move, introduced me to a meditative prayer practice. But more than that, it revealed layers of unrest and confusion about my place in the world. While I walked the circles, the sensation of being helplessly lost stirred familiar anxiety, and I began to realize something bigger was afoot than a simple stroll through a labyrinth. I could see the destination—the three benches in the inner circle—but I couldn't understand why some of the circuits were taking me away from the center rather than toward it. In some moments, the labyrinth began to feel like the maze of traffic we were navigating each day, itself a symbol of the mid-life disruption of my husband's job being downsized in New York, and our family starting over again in a place we'd never expected to live.

As I put one foot in front of the other, I discovered that, unlike a maze full of false starts and dead ends like a complicated puzzle needing to be solved, the labyrinth was doing the work of orientation *for* me. Each turn eventually resolved itself toward the center and I only needed to keep walking the pathway, rounding each bend until, to my amazement, I stood in the quiet center of the circle. When it was time to return, I pointed myself back toward the entrance, and the path led me out. As I slowly made the circuitous journey in toward the center and back out again, I felt my mind, heart, and body shift from anxiety to rest.

Somehow, this experience of prayer within the simple borders of historically meaningful architecture opened me to hearing new invitations from Jesus to follow his restful way in the middle of a disruptive world. My introduction to spiritual practices like the prayer labyrinth became one of the "ancient paths" that reoriented my soul in a season of profound disorientation. It was as if the retreat grounds in Texas came with an invitation: "All you who are weary from ill-fitting roadways and burdensome traffic, come in. Walk my simple pathways and learn a restful way to travel."

The invitation to walk a restful path in the company of Jesus felt meaningful in the quiet consolation of a retreat center, but for the invitation to be a lasting gift it needed to bear the weight of the burdens of the *outside* world. I needed to leave the retreat center and return home to my family, who were all suffering their own versions of the anxious fatigue that my time in prayer and silence had revealed in me. Once again, the Texas roadways provide a metaphor for our lives in this season. As much as I tried to avoid it, there was no way of living in Austin, Texas, without entering the concrete maze of I-35 many times a week, thus provoking another bout of anxious disorientation and more cursing than I've ever done in my life. What I needed more than an occasional contemplative spiritual retreat was a new way to travel that lightened my load, rather than buried me under it. I needed the steady rhythms of the prayer path to form me into a freer, lighter person walking through my actual everyday life.

I was first introduced to the spiritual practice of a Rule of Life shortly after another disruptive cross-country move—another job for my pastor husband, this time in Connecticut and none of our children coming with us. I moved back east a little older and wiser, yet once again wholly disoriented in a new season of life. Gathering with our new church community helped. The regular rhythms of our Sunday liturgy and the natural transitions of once again living in the four seasons of the northeastern United States helped. But this new season of an empty nest, without the familiar patterns of family life, introduced me to particular, profound grief. Like I'd heard from many others who had experienced this stage of parenting before me, I felt utterly *lost*. My relational landscape had completely changed, and I began to wonder if I would ever feel at home in my own home again.

Once again, God led me to the old pathways of spiritual disciplines to help me find my footing in our new community. Within a few months of our arrival in Connecticut, at the invitation of another pastor's wife, I began a two-year certificate course in spiritual direction. It was during this training that I was first introduced to the Rule of Life as a discipline available to regular Christians rather than just monks. I learned that, for centuries, Christian monastic communities have used this practice to organize Jesus' most life-giving invitations and greatest commands into shared patterns of daily prayer, work, relationships, and rest. Through their teaching and example, I was being invited to step into a pathway where, instead of the inevitable disruptions to our life delivering us to a dead end like a maze, we begin to discern patterns and rhythms of our life in the company of Jesus. Rather than a to-do list or a self-help tool, a Rule of Life gathers up the fragmented bits of our lives and reintegrates us in the restful way of Jesus. I didn't understand all of this at first, but I was being invited to a life-giving spiritual practice, a spacious path for my weary soul.

First, I learned the history. The Rule of Life as a spiritual practice is mainly credited to Saint Benedict of Nursia[3]. He was a fifth-century Christian who later became a well-known and celebrated saint. Benedictine monasteries worldwide grew out of Benedict's search for a way of following Jesus in the religiously and politically turbulent early Middle Ages. He grew up in a life of privilege, became disillusioned, pursued academia, and then quickly discovered that his desire for a purposeful life was not matched by the other students in his community, who seemed to be inclined more toward drunken partying.[4]

Benedict left the world of academia before he really knew what he wanted to do next. Prompted by disillusionment with all the other ways he'd tried to seek a life of prayer and purpose, he decided to strip it all away to seek God's will for his life. He was drawn toward solitude and spent approximately three years living in a small cave so that he could prayerfully listen for God's direction.[5] Three years later, he emerged with clarity of purpose for not only his life but for a community of Christ-followers who would eventually change the face of the Christian community in the world. His rule would take time to formally develop what we now know as the seventy-three chapters of the Rule of Saint Benedict[6], but during his time in the cave he had simply discerned that God's will for him was to live a humble life shaped by contemplation and community. The foundational elements of a Rule of Life—prayer, work, study, hospitality, and rest—would all spring from this twofold call.

After learning the history, I began to read how normal people like me applied the Benedictine rule to their lives. I read that a Rule of Life is a spiritual practice of discerning and recording Jesus' invitations for my life, then ordering my daily, monthly, and yearly commitments into an integrated Rule with the desire to follow Jesus consistently and gratefully. I began to appreciate the scope of Benedict's rule, which brilliantly synthesizes the way of life Jesus gives us in scripture, detailed enough to apply to all of life yet spacious enough to contextualize every age. Even though his rule was written for use in a monastic community, as a framework for living the two greatest commandments Jesus gave us—to love the Lord with all our heart, soul, and mind, and to love our neighbors as ourselves (Luke 10:25–28)—his rule creates a pathway for us to follow as we seek to live in the loving, restful way of Jesus.

This is how I've come to understand the practice of a Rule, but it is not how I started.

A RULE OF LIFE AS A SPACIOUS PATH

I began creating a Rule of Life during my first spiritual direction residency. The book we had been assigned to help us in the task suggested the copious making of lists—of our relationships, values, skills, hopes, disciplines, and constraints—that all became fodder for a master list to form our Rule of Life. At the intellectual level, this method made sense. We could prayerfully recall and examine our highest responsibilities and deepest values to create a database from which to select the practices and habits we would keep each day, month, and year as a Rule of Life.

I've been making lists and keeping journals since childhood, so my initial response to the assignment was enthusiastic. But that instinct didn't last long. Instead of feeling energized as I reviewed my journals and began creating inventories of my relationships, roles, and responsibilities, I froze, remembering that I am actually terrible at living my life according to what I write down on paper. Sitting in front of a workbook to help me organize my life in categories to complete the assignment of writing a Rule of Life prompted this old inner tension. Somewhere along the way between childhood and mid-life— as choices became more complex, energy more limited, and disappointments more acute—my love for lists became associated with shame and cynicism. Where I'd first approached the Rule of Life exercise with optimism and expectancy, I now felt despair. The voice in my head said, "Why set yourself up for failure? Just write something down to complete the assignment and move on."

I felt embarrassed to admit to anyone in my training cohort that I was not enjoying the assignment. Gradually, I learned I was not the only one struggling with the project, and I wondered why, out of all the spiritual practices we were learning, this one seemed to stymie us. None of us were questioning the practice itself. We were prone to accepting historical and spiritual disciplines; we were in training because we believed in them so deeply. For some of us, the struggle seemed to be about the method. Somehow the list-making wasn't reaching our hearts, and this felt especially surprising since the work of spiritual direction is to encourage people to integrate their thoughts, feelings, and behaviors in following Jesus.

As I learned from teachers, listened to the Holy Spirit with my spiritual director, and talked about the practice of a Rule of Life with friends, I began to understand that while list-making is a helpful place for many folks to start, it was just a tiny (and somewhat optional) part of the practice. I needed to begin creating a Rule of Life not from list-making but from listening to Jesus, others, and my own soul, and I did not know how to listen in a loving way.

So I began there: making space to listen and, along with my spiritual direction supervisor, to regularly, lovingly reflect on what I noticed in the listening. This led to my second important discovery about why my initial understanding of the Rule of Life as a spiritual practice felt so frustrating and fruitless. My early attempts at self-inventory were self-referential. Yes, I was praying, but all the material I had to work with and the outcomes I anticipated from the practice began and ended with my own discernment and evaluation. I needed the companionship of other people to help me listen to my own life.

As I grew in my capacity for prayerful listening and loving presence with myself and others, the Rule of Life became not a restrictive requirement but a spacious invitation to follow the restful way of Jesus. Instead of cynicism that weighed down my ability to hope, I began to sense a lightness in my expectations for myself and others, and instead of shame, I began to feel the freedom to practice a Rule as my imperfect, but true self in the company of Jesus and others. Over the years, documenting a Rule of Life has become an archive of transformation instead of another method of recording my failures to stick to a plan.

Like the geometric precision of the labyrinth offering a path to walk in restful and rewarding rhythms, the Rule of Life has offered a similar rubric of structure and rhythms for weary and disjointed Christian communities for fifteen centuries. As a reader who picked up this book, I assume you are at least curious about spiritual practices and that you may have questions about the merit or methods of keeping a Rule of Life. Christian spiritual practices, like prayer, are an open invitation for anyone desiring to draw nearer to Jesus. If that describes your desire, then you are in the right place. Welcome!

You might also sense some hesitation or embarrassment about your previous attempts to order your life around spiritual practices. I can't remove every bit of resistance you may feel, but I hope in these pages you will find that the rewards outweigh the costs of working through whatever hang-ups you might bring with you to this practice. If you've gotten this far through the introduction, that's worth noticing as an invitation to risk beginning again. Spiritual practice is, after all, another way to say discipline. And for many, that's not a positive word because a discipline, by definition, requires us to grow and change. Disciplines stretch us in sometimes uncomfortable ways, but, thankfully, we are not responsible for the outcomes—only the willingness to be open to Jesus. Spiritual disciplines expand us, making space for the Holy Spirit to make us more spacious, open, receptive to God's love, wisdom, and action in our lives.

In his book *Celebration of Discipline: The Path to Spiritual Growth*, Richard Foster describes the purpose of spiritual practices, or disciplines, this way:

> A farmer is helpless to grow grain; all he can do is provide the right conditions for the growing of grain. He cultivates the ground, he plants the seed, he waters the plants, and then the natural forces of the earth take over and up comes the grain. This is the way it is with the Spiritual Disciplines—they are a way of sowing to the Spirit. By themselves the Spiritual Disciplines can do nothing; they can only get us to the place where something can be done.[7]

The same is true for practicing the spiritual discipline of a Rule of Life—by itself, it can't draw us closer to Jesus. The exercise may provide peace of mind and order to our days, but the essential purpose is to create space for Jesus to become evident to you and through you. And like other disciplines, such as silence, worship, and hospitality, we don't make the practice, the practice makes us. The transformative power of spiritual practices is nothing we initiate; it's a gift we can receive.

No matter where you are in your spiritual journey and where you call your spiritual home, there are (at least) five transformative gifts we have already received as followers of Christ that create the groundwork for the spacious path of a Rule of Life. I've come to think of the following list as incredible realities that make it possible to follow the restful way of Jesus in a fragmented world.

1. We are rooted and grounded in the love of Jesus, who is the embodied revelation of God's love. A Rule of Life is a spacious path to seek and find God's love, because through the invitations of Jesus, God's love sought and found us first. (1 John 4:19)

2. We are given everything we need to live like Jesus, who fulfilled all of God's requirements—primarily to love God and to love our neighbors as ourselves. A Rule of Life is a spacious path to prayerfully listen to and lovingly embody all that Jesus says is necessary for our lives. (Romans 13:8–10)

3. We are called to travel together following one triune God, who offers one baptism into the beloved Father, Son, and Holy Spirit. A Rule of Life is a spacious path for our true identity found in the unity of diversity in God's beloved community. (Ephesians 4:1–6)

4. We live with Christ as fully-formed humans, blessed once in our creation as the image of God, and forever when Jesus became one of us. A Rule of Life is a spacious path to live one integrated life as an act of worship because Jesus reconciled us with God

and blesses every inherent tension of living in God's
kingdom. (Romans 12:1–2)

5. We live with the Holy Spirit in the present, in the
    power of God who is always making things new.
    (Revelation 21:22) A Rule of Life is a spacious path
    to begin again and again because Christ has died,
    Christ is risen, and Christ will come again.[8]

It bears repeating: a Rule of Life doesn't initiate any of this
work. The Rule of Life builds on the groundwork already laid,
because the Holy Spirit is alive in us continually making us
more like Jesus and more like the true self God has always
imagined us to be.

As language and cultural norms shift through time, spiritual disciplines that have been handed down to us through the
history of the church are all liable to misunderstanding, and
the Rule of Life is no exception. Along with these five incredible realities, I have summarized a series of misconceptions that
create the most stubborn obstacles to understanding the Rule
as a spacious path. The first is about the name of the discipline
itself and is tricky enough to warrant a few pages here at the
beginning of the book.

First, we need to talk about the word *rule*. This word is, perhaps, the most frequently-mentioned hesitation when it comes
to practicing a Rule of Life: there must be a better name for
this discipline. Let's be honest, Benedict didn't have to worry
about the same public relations concerns we do in the twenty-
first century. Although we as a culture are often okay with
rules for diet, exercise, time management, and athletic events,
rules for spiritual living are definitely not in vogue. On top of
that, the institution of the church is entangled with oppressive
laws and systemic injustice throughout history. As a result, *rule*

implies those in power coercing and crushing those beneath them. Maybe there *is* a better name for this discipline—and I've heard several good options—but whatever you decide to call this practice, it's important to understand the purpose of the original language to receive the full formational gift of this historic Christian discipline.

The phrase *Rule of Life* is literally translated from the original Latin *regula vitae,* but the meaning has shifted through the centuries. In its original state, *regula* refers to a specific pattern in ancient Greek architectural design.[9] Where our modern ears hear "rule" and think "requirement of the law," the etymology invites us to hear "rule" and think "repeated architectural pattern." This is a much more spacious and fluid interpretation of a word that we often associate with strict and inflexible.

A Rule of Life understood through the language of Jesus' invitation in Matthew 11:28–30 (*The Message*) reminds us that Jesus is inviting us into a way of living that is not ill-fitting, heavy, or burdensome. Comparing the Matthew 11 definition of the "easy yoke" of Jesus to our understanding of a restful way of life is hard enough. For those who have experienced oppression or abuse, the word *rule* can mean something harsh and deadly.

As I've practiced a Rule of Life, I've paid attention to the resistance from my companions (and sometimes from myself) to living life by a Rule. Sometimes, resistance is a natural reflex to counter anything threatening our idea of autonomy. Sometimes, the resistance is a prophetic call against systems of oppression enacted by those with the power to rule over others. Our Western religious expression thrived unchecked for centuries on an understanding of itself in terms of Anglo male supremacy, and Saint Benedict's day was no different. Benedict began his life in the aristocracy, full of privilege.

His choice to give up his wealth to become poor was an exercise of personal agency, a choice that only a privileged life affords.[10]

On this tension, I find the words of author and Benedictine nun Joan Chittister helpful:

> The Rule of Benedict called the class-centered Roman world to community and calls us to the same on a globe that is fragmented. The rule called for hospitality in times of barbarian invasions and calls us to care in a world of neighborhood strangers. It called for equality in a society full of classes and castes and calls us to equality in a world that proclaims everyone equal but judges everyone differently. Benedict, who challenged the patriarchal society of Rome to humility, challenges our own world, too . . .[11]

In Benedict's countercultural call away from the "classes and castes" thriving not only in Roman society but also in the Roman church, he subverted the older monastic ideals. These ideals centered on individuals known as "holy men" who issued edicts for others to follow within little cells of isolation or, in the case of novice monastics, gathered at the feet of a "rule master." For Benedict, the community's relationship took precedence over the power of one leader. According to Benedictine scholar Esther de Waal, "St. Benedict changes this almost exclusively vertical pattern of authority by emphasizing the relationships of the monks with each other." While leader and follower, trainer and trainee, discipler and disciple had their place in Benedict's rule, he nurtured an ethos defined as a community "bound in love to each other."[12] With its origins rooted in the structures that nurture relationship, the phrase *Rule of Life* becomes a loving invitation to follow in the footsteps of this community bound in love.

In addition to misunderstandings about the meaning of the word "rule," here are five more misconceptions that hinder us from practicing a Rule of Life as a spacious path.

1. A Rule of Life is not a new system to initiate spiritual growth on our own terms but rather makes space to say yes to Jesus' invitations to unforced rhythms of freedom and commitment.

2. A Rule of Life is not a spiritualized method for self-determination but rather makes space to prayerfully discern and lovingly embody all that God commands.

3. A Rule of Life is not a way to promote a false religious version of ourselves but rather makes space for our true selves to find rest within the beloved, baptized community of the triune God.

4. A Rule of Life is not a way to perpetuate idealized versions of our work and worship but rather makes space to offer our everyday lives as an act of worship to the God who is present to us in the reality of our lives.

5. A Rule of Life is not a map for continual upward movement toward a vision of spiritual maturity but rather makes space for us to embrace the challenges that upend our lives as the creative tensions of God's kingdom, blessed and empowered by the Holy Spirit who is always making things new.

My hope for this book is to help us not only reframe these misconceptions but, in the process, to encourage us to grow in our capacity to listen to and love Jesus, others, and ourselves.

You may be tempted along the way to use the Rule of Life for any number of the misconceived versions I've mentioned.

I've found the strongest temptation to be to retreat into the false narrative and self-protection of a Jesus-and-me existence. It is true that we live with Christ in us *and* also in a community that helps us listen to the direction of the Holy Spirit. This reality—Jesus and community—is essential to the practice of a Rule.

As I write this book, the world is emerging from years of collective disruption, learning how to redefine normal. What I was feeling after our move to Austin seems small in comparison to the profound disorientation of global upheaval. We long for the familiar roads of our old lives to help us navigate the complicated maze of a post-pandemic world. A Pew Research Poll from March 2022 states, "A growing share of Americans appear ready to move on to a new normal, even as the exact contours . . . are hard to discern." The same poll states that, despite the desire and resources to help us move into a post-pandemic life, much of our "landscape still feels unsettled."[13] Whether on a personal scale or at the global level, cycles of change and disruption tend to create an increasing sense of disorientation as familiar pathways crumble and often result in fragmented relationships with God, others, and our own souls. Our relationships, rhythms, and trusted institutions may seem inadequate or, worse, unavailable to help us with our actual daily needs and desires. But in this reality, our lives share a common theme with Jesus and centuries of his followers. When Jesus offered the stunning invitation to come to him to learn how to live and work from a place of rest, he was talking to people weighed down by ill-fitting political, economic, and religious systems.

In the context of our collective disruption, it feels risky to invite you to an ancient Christian practice called a Rule of Life. Even riskier to call the practice a spacious path. I don't want you to feel like I've created a bait-and-switch tactic with the title of this book. There's a tension here that goes deeper than reframing old language to describe spiritual disciplines or anecdotes about frustrating city infrastructure. At the heart of this book, I'm inviting you to explore the tension with me. What does it mean to live in the freedom of God's love while also desiring to follow God's laws? How can we live every day in the reality that the path of following begins with a narrow gate yet delivers us to a spacious place? (Matthew 7:13–14).

The Hebrew root for "spacious place"—*merchâb*—is related to the biblical use of the word *salvation*.[14] We see this when the psalmist talks about being put in a wide-open place, surprised by the spaciousness and the reality of being loved. This word—which means "broad or roomy place" or "wide expanses"—is repeated all through the Psalms:

"When hard pressed, I cried to the LORD; he brought me into a spacious place" (Psalm 118:5).

"You have not given me into the hands of the enemy but have set my feet in a spacious place" (Psalm 31:8).

" . . . yet you have brought us out to a spacious place" (Psalm 66:12, NRSVue).

And, my favorite, "He brought me out into a spacious place; he rescued me because he delighted in me" (Psalm 18:19). We hear echoes of this broad place in *The Message* version of Romans 5:2: "We find ourselves standing where we always hoped we might stand—out in the wide open spaces of God's grace and glory, standing tall and shouting our praise."

This is the ground we are standing on when we practice a Rule of Life, and it's why I find the phrase *spacious path* so compelling. It combines the vast dimensions of God's love with the ingredients of salvation rescue—cruciform love and human limitations. Jesus holds all this together in his life, death, resurrection, ascension, and promise to return again bringing with him the fullness of God's new creation. In practicing a Rule of Life, we root ourselves in his love. *He* is the ground we stand on. As Esther de Waal says, we "aim to live a life that is earthed in Christ."[15] The spacious path of a Rule of Life helps us practice living a life that is earthed in Christ until the day our resurrected feet are firmly planted in the new earth of our forever home.

As we move forward together in this book, I pray for us Paul's words, that God would "strengthen you by his Spirit—not a brute strength but a glorious inner strength—that Christ will live in you as you open the door and invite him in. And I ask him that with both feet planted firmly on love, you'll be able to take in with all followers of Jesus the extravagant dimensions of Christ's love. Reach out and experience the breadth! Test its length! Plumb the depths! Rise to the heights! Live full lives, full in the fullness of God" (Ephesians 3:16–19, *The Message*). Amen.

Walk with me, friends, on the spacious path.

ENTERING THE SPACIOUS PATH OF A RULE OF LIFE: HOW TO GET THE MOST OUT OF THIS BOOK

In the coming chapters, I hope to offer the personal, pastoral, and practical guidance that will help us find our bearings in forming and practicing a Rule of Life. Along the way, I'll suggest simple but meaningful practices of listening and love suited to the actual shape of our lives right now—disrupted and disoriented though they may be. More than that, I hope to provide companionship in book form that you can return to again and again as you seek to embrace the spacious and simple path of the Rule of Life while your life continues to change and grow.

Throughout the book, you'll notice I repeatedly use the metaphor of a prayer labyrinth as the illustration I've found most helpful for imagining a Rule of Life as a spacious path. My first experience with a labyrinth was far more intuitive than my first effort at practicing a Rule of Life. With its circular rhythms and imaginative architecture, many people describe feeling an almost "instant rapport" with a labyrinth. Perhaps we could think of a prayer labyrinth as the approachable, easy-to-talk-to person at the cocktail party and the Rule of Life as the "great once you get to know them" person. Every good party makes space for both.

Components of a prayer labyrinth—like the ground, entrance, pathway, borders, and center—frame the chapters and practices of the book. We'll begin at the entrance, with the invitation to the spiritual practice of a Rule of Life as a spacious path to seeking God in the company of Jesus, others, and our own souls. As we begin walking the path, we'll recognize the importance of the borders that structure the path, always guiding us so that we can remain focused on our destination: the center of the labyrinth. We'll explore how the twofold calling of a Rule of Life—contemplation and community—mimic the borders of a pathway, helping us to grow in discernment through the everyday practices of prayerful listening and embodied presence that orient our lives toward God's love. We'll consider the center of the spacious path, the place we arrive again and again, as the place we find our truest selves, centered in the belovedness of God. Reoriented and named as one of the beloved community of Jesus, we'll consider how the borders of the spacious path guide us inward and outward from the center place of our truest selves in communion with

God's beloved. We'll talk about rhythms of relational commitments and tensions of holding all the parts of our lives together
like the repeating circuits of a labyrinth—sometimes feeling
open and pleasant and other times feeling like they're pointing
us in exactly the wrong direction from where we thought we
were headed. These components are essential to practicing a
Rule of Life, and they all find meaning from the beloved center
of God's love. In the last chapter, we'll welcome St. Benedict's
prayer: "Always we begin again." Returning to the center and
making ourselves at home in God's love is what following the
restful way of Jesus is all about.

Whether the practice of a Rule of Life is brand new to you
or you are someone who has gotten stuck along the way, know
that I understand, and that you are welcome here. If you're
currently practicing a Rule of Life and are reading for a little
bit of encouragement or maybe to find a way to share this
practice with your community, I'm so glad you're here. May
all of us know we are held together in the beloved Father, Son,
and Holy Spirit, and hear Jesus' invitations for rest along the
spacious path.

But first I need to tell you about the time I tried—and
failed—to live like a monk.

BEGINNING

The Bible isn't about people trying to discover God, but about God reaching out to find us.

—JOHN STOTT[1]

Love has taught the soul to travel Love's paths, and the soul has followed them faithfully . . .

—BEATRICE OF NAZARETH[2]

Sometimes—perhaps most times—the plans I concoct for my spiritual formation spring from an ideal that I've harbored, often unknowingly, for what a spiritual life *should* look or feel like. Sometimes—perhaps most times—my experience of prayer and spiritual practices turns out nothing like my ideals. This has been true my whole life, but no experience illustrates my stubborn tendency for idealized versions of spiritual practices better than our stay at a Benedictine monastery in Ireland in 2016.

SEEKING AND BEING FOUND

Let me begin at the beginning. For our twenty-fifth wedding anniversary, our kids raised money to send Brian and me to

Ireland. They called it our second honeymoon, and since our first honeymoon was in a little town in Pennsylvania just a short drive from home, our friends and family rallied to give us a trip to remember. Plus, they knew we were headed into a physically taxing and emotionally intense season and that by the time we could take the trip, we'd be pretty tired. In the first six months following our anniversary and leading up to the date we selected for our trip to Ireland, we celebrated our son's wedding, our youngest child's high school graduation, Brian's ordination into the priesthood, and my final weeks working full-time at an Austin digital advertising company. In the middle of all those events and more, we interviewed for and accepted a job across the country, packed up our house in Austin, and cried many, many tears with our kids who had, understandably, assumed if anyone was going to move away it would be them, at the beginning of their adulthoods, and not their parents in the middle of theirs. Planning for our second honeymoon became a kind of comforting dreamscape for me during all the emotional upheaval of those six months.

Knowing we'd be headed from one full ministry season into another in our new congregation, we decided to devote one week of our trip to more traditional sabbatical activities— prayer, study, contemplation, and silence. In my search for a place to retreat, I discovered a ninety-year-old Benedictine community living behind the replicated walls of a twelfth-century castle on the southwest coast of Ireland. Perfect. They had a room available the week we needed it that met our budget—pay what you can. Better than perfect. It felt a bit risky to make the reservation since we are not monastics, nor are we Roman Catholic. Exhaustion made me feel a bit desperate, which is often what I feel when I create plans for prayer and spiritual renewal, so I shoved aside any doubts that this experience could possibly turn out differently than I had imagined. We decided to take the reputation of Benedictine hospitality seriously and hope they would welcome two married American Protestants.

On our first day, we arrived at the monastery at 3:00 p.m., and by 7:00 p.m., I'd been scolded by a monk—twice.[3] My dream of a blissful spiritual experience began to crumble the moment we met the guest master, whom I'll call Father Donovan. We had followed the directions to our guest house, parked the car, and moved toward the front doors as quickly as possible under the weight of our luggage and high expectations. The doors didn't open, and we discovered we were locked out. The woman at the main desk assured us that Father Donovan would meet us there. We pushed the doorbell, eager to begin our week of prayerful devotion.

While we waited, I practically pressed my face against the glass door, but with my first glimpse of Father Donovan, I began to worry. I noticed that the monk did not seem very excited to see us. When he got to the door, he opened it halfway, asked us who we were, and paused, I felt, as if to evaluate our sincerity. My excitement to be staying at a monastery overpowered my typically guarded personality. At that moment Father Donovan stood between me and the pursuit of my goal for a week of prayerful devotion, beginning—according to my itinerary—at the monastery's acclaimed icon chapel. Before the monk could decide what to do with us, I blurted, "The woman at the front desk told us you'd give me directions to the icon chapel?" The color on his ruddy cheeks turned almost crimson, "Oh, of course, she did. Isn't that just the way it always goes?"

I blinked, unsure of how to respond. Father Donovan— still holding the door half shut—launched into a monologue, lamenting the failure of his energy level to keep up with the demands others made upon his time. Still undaunted, I interrupted the monk's tirade, "We'll be here for a whole week, so we have plenty of time if you'd rather take us later." I'd seen the images of the icon chapel on the abbey website, I gushed, and I hoped to spend hours there contemplating the mysteries of God's presence. Father Donovan harrumphed and finally allowed us to enter.

Things went downhill from there. Since I couldn't visit the icon chapel right away, I consoled myself with the next two items on my bucket list: daily prayer services in the ornate sanctuary and visits to the monastery library. But when I arrived at Vespers—ready to listen to Gregorian chant, surrounded by the aroma of incense in a beautiful marbled sanctuary—the first thing I saw was a large placard announcing that, following the service, the building would be closed indefinitely for major construction. Two strikes: no icon chapel or church sanctuary for daily prayer services. At least I'd still have the library, I thought, as I mumbled my amens in all the right places of the liturgy while calculating how I would carry all the books I wanted back to our room after the service was over.

Thankfully, the library door was not locked when I rushed in after the prayer service. I wandered from shelf to shelf, not knowing where to begin. I was utterly alone in the building and nearly giddy in the presence of so many books. With a week of unscheduled time ahead of me (minus the time I'd spend in prayer, of course) I figured I could tackle a stack tall enough to reach my eyeballs. I began accumulating books from the poetry section: Seamus Heaney and Yeats, of course, and James Joyce because I'd still never read him. I made one trip to the desk in the front of the room to set down an armload of books before returning to the shelves. While I searched for Thomas Merton's titles, I heard the door on the other side of the room creak open. I shook off the curious instinct to hide and stepped out of the stacks to meet Father Donovan's gaze. I noticed his cheeks were crimson again.

"May I ask what you are doing here?"

"Just looking through the books," I heard my unnaturally bright voice respond. I didn't mention the stack I'd already lifted off the shelves. "My husband and I are staying at the monastery for a week." I wrongly assumed this would be enough explanation.

He cleared his throat. "The library is for the community."

I was relieved to hear this. "Yes, we're guests. We're staying in your guesthouse for a whole week." I wondered how Father Donovan had already forgotten me. This was the third time I found myself reminding him we were planning to stay in his guesthouse for a week. He stared back, looking uncomfortable. I said, "Oh. When you say community, you mean the *monks*?"

Of course, the monks. He didn't speak the words out loud, but I could see it in his eyes. He hesitated and then asked, in what felt to me like an obligatory way, "Is there a book you need?"

I answered in my phony-bright voice, "Oh, no. I don't need any books! I have *loads* of books in my room already." I noticed my tone had shifted from childlike gushing to something that sounded almost arrogant, as if my carry-on suitcase could compare to the centuries-old collection in the room behind me. Father Donovan turned toward the exit, and I stood frozen in place trying to hold back angry tears until I saw his black robe sweep through the outer door. I wiped my face, and with a vindictive flair, I left the books I'd collected in a heap on the desk for some unsuspecting monk to sort out later.

I returned to our room, threw myself onto my single bed in our monastic cell, and sobbed to my husband who was resting on his single bed across the room: "I want to go home!" If this experience wasn't going to match the vision in my head of unrestricted access to the accoutrements of monastic prayer—uninterrupted silence, transcendent worship services, and meaningful conversations with inspiring monks—then I wanted to quit.

As you may have guessed, we didn't leave. I want to say the week improved after that, but it didn't.

At breakfast the following morning, Father Donovan snapped at Brian for taking only enough milk out of the refrigerator for his own bowl of cereal: "We try to run a civilized kitchen here," he said as he poured the milk into an ornate silver pitcher to place on the table for everyone's use. Prayer services were canceled without notice, we found padlocks on gardens we had hoped to roam, and we somehow continued to annoy Father Donovan in spite of our best intentions.

About midweek, as I resigned myself to the fact that I may as well make the best of our situation, I selected a book from my suitcase. Before we left home, I had grabbed this unread title off my shelf because I vaguely remembered that in it, Kathleen Norris wrote about her experience visiting a Benedictine monastery in the United States. Weeks ago, I couldn't have known I would need this American Protestant woman to explain to me the quirks of a monastic community. As I read, I began to understand Father Donovan in a new way. Norris explained, "Saint Benedict, writing in the sixth century, notes that a monastery is never without guests and admonishes monks to 'receive all guests as Christ.' Monks have quickly recognized that such hospitality, undoubtedly a blessing, can also create burdens for them."[4]

I decided then that I'd still avoid Father Donovan, but not out of fear as much as a desire to ease his burden of hospitality.

We'd discovered another garden—one that was not pad-locked, thankfully—hidden behind stone archways and pro-tected by leafy tree branches, where we began to go before breakfast each morning, carrying our prayer book and a thermos of hot tea. The first morning we did this, I barely noticed our surroundings. We sat on a wrought iron bench, surrounded by bursts of colorful midsummer flowers, but I couldn't pray because—I'm embarrassed to admit this—I was annoyed that there was no Gregorian chant in the garden, no bells or flickering candles. But I sat anyway, hoping the feeling would pass and I would become even the littlest bit grateful. I knew my anxious and irritated reactions to the unexpected, yet still beautiful, surroundings could not possibly be all that God intended for me to experience while we were here, so I tried to turn my disappointment in prayer.

Eventually, as my body began to settle in the quiet, I noticed the soft patter of a single stream of water from the stone fountain at the center of the garden. I walked to the fountain, enjoying the aromatic lilies, roses, and foxgloves, listening to water and the swallows greeting the day. I began to feel some-thing like gratitude. This garden was beautiful, and I'd been welcomed into it—not to check off a monastic bucket list, but for prayer and rest in a place where prayer "has been valid," as T. S. Eliot coined in his "Little Gidding."[5] In that same poem, Eliot found gratitude for his own awkward pilgrimage with the admonition, "You are here to kneel." I'd read the words earlier in our prayer book, and they returned to me now as an invitation. In the trickling of a water fountain and the words of an old poet, I finally heard the invitation of Jesus. "Keep me company, Tamara. Watch and pray with me."

For the rest of the week, Brian and I walked each morning to the walled garden carrying our prayer book. By day five, I noticed a hint of admiration in Father Donovan's eyes when he asked at breakfast where we had been already, so early in the morning. In turn, I began to look at Father Donovan in a new way. I noticed how seriously he took his responsibility to serve the morning meal. While waiting together over a boiling egg, I listened to him describe his daily routine of procuring home-made soda bread, eggs for poaching, and bowls of fresh fruit from the monastery farm and kitchen. Throughout the day, he washed the remnants of the dirtied teacups left by guests and prepared the Crock-Pot for porridge. He filled pottery with gooseberry and currant jam he made from berries he picked in the (padlocked) monastery garden each afternoon and set the table with china and linen every night after Compline. I began to understand why the guest master noticed even a single teacup was out of place. This kitchen was his prayer garden, where he walked a pathway each morning and evening.

On our last evening, after we helped prepare berries for the next morning's jam, Father Donovan took us on a tour of the icon chapel in the church's crypt where he instructed us on the story of each image. After all the times I'd heard him mutter sarcastically, I was shocked to discover that he was an eloquent and passionate docent. This display moved us, and we were silent—almost prayerful—without being asked. It was not the long hours of adoration I'd hoped for when I imagined myself in an icon chapel, but it was a meaningful moment in another important way. In the holy air of the underground icon chapel, I felt—for a few brief moments—part of this community of monks.

During our final breakfast with Father Donovan, I joyfully scooped jewel-red currant jam I'd helped prepare onto homemade Irish bread and listened to the monk discuss theology, politics, and the proper method of a coffee press. We had arrived wanting mystic euphoria and instead received time to sleep, read, study, pray for our new congregation waiting for us in Connecticut, eat Irish porridge, and learn humility. Kathleen Norris taught me empathy, T. S. Eliot admonished my contrarian spirit, Father Donovan helped me imagine the real life of a monk, and my husband, with the prayer book and tea, helped me to pray. And not least of all, Jesus invited me to enter the real work of the abbey—to kneel where prayer had been valid. I'd entered as a spiritual tourist and left a grateful guest.[6]

The tension between spiritual idealism and simple gratitude for the actual life I'm living is one of the most frequent challenges I face in practicing a Rule of Life. On any given day, I approach the habits and practices written in my rule like a tourist's bucket list rather than the invitations of God to simply form and sustain me—body and soul. Like our visit to the monastery, I want the Rule I've created to deliver outcomes of mystic euphoria and profound spiritual insight and, in the process, I am prone to miss the presence of God I say that I'm seeking. With the eyes of a tourist, I am blinded to the gift of Jesus' companionship. I can only see my own ideals and expectations. But if I pay attention—even, and maybe especially, in those moments of despairing disappointment—I will hear a gentle summons to notice God and to notice myself in God. With practice in the company of Jesus and others, I've discovered that seeking and finding God isn't about a pursuit, but about an invitation into God's presence. In the same way, practicing a Rule of Life is not the end goal or even the means to pursuing an end goal. The end and the means are all found in a person: Jesus Christ.

BUT WE HAD HOPED

Following Jesus' crucifixion, two disciples walk the Emmaus Road toward Jerusalem, according to Luke 24:13-31. As they walk and talk, a stranger appears out of nowhere to join them. In true hospitable fashion, the stranger is invited to join the conversation over dinner where the two friends summarize their disappointment at the way things ended in four words: "But we had hoped." A Rule of Life helps us to give voice to what we have learned, what we had hoped for, and what we are grieving. We welcome the stranger. We tend to the movements of our hearts stirring within us; we feed our bodies on bread and wine. And for heaven's sake, we don't do any of this alone.

They had pressed their face to the glass of Jesus' audacious claims and miraculous healings, and now Jesus was dead. Nothing was turning out the way they'd expected. The words they said to the stranger who showed up to walk with them on the road—"But we had hoped . . ."—evoke the moments of spiritual disillusionment most of us have experienced. The good news is, Jesus doesn't leave them in despair. Once bread is broken, their eyes are opened to the reality sitting right before them. Then, Jesus is gone as suddenly as he appeared.

Walking, talking, and breaking bread with the Emmaus travelers isn't the only time Jesus surprises his friends by showing up unannounced and leaving the same way. In fact, we recognize in him the God who arrives in so many of our well-known Bible stories: as a flame in a burning bush, a still small voice in a cave, and three guests who show up for dinner to an unexpecting Abram and Sarai. But of all the ways God arrives, none was more surprising than the choice to take the form of a human. Jesus is not only the most unexpected arrival of God but the most intimate revelation of God. No longer requiring a mystical disguise, Jesus lived on the earth, and for thirty-three years of human history, God could be seen, touched, and smelled. God was someone who could be birthed, embraced, and killed.

In Luke 24, we read that even though Jesus himself came near to the disciples, their eyes "were kept from recognizing him." This God who will soon knock Saul off his horse in a blinding light on the Damascus road is the same God who also dims the eyes of those who are longing to see Jesus on the Emmaus road. With the resurrected Jesus, we begin again to read the mysterious revelations of God's presence as he spends a few weeks demonstrating the stunning realities of a resurrected body. He wants to remind them also that, in order to recognize God, we have to remain open to a little bit of mystery. My pastor once said that maybe Jesus stayed on earth a few weeks after the resurrection to remind his friends that, although resurrected, he was still human. Even though he would need to go away again, Jesus demonstrated in explicitly human ways that he loved them. God loves us, too, and while we cannot touch and hear and smell Jesus, we are also his friends. We need to be open to mystery, and train our senses to recognize all the ways God arrives among us.

Filipino artist Emmanuel Garibay[7] draws the Emmaus dinner scene in a completely unexpected approach that helps us enter the deeper layers of meaning in the Emmaus story. Bottles of beer replace the chalice we might expect to see in the painting, but we understand we're imagining the familiar story of Jesus revealing himself to his grieving friends. In Garibay's depiction, we seem to be entering the room a few seconds after the Emmaus travelers understand they were eating a meal with their friend Jesus. They are laughing and smacking their foreheads in the shock of recognition. We imagine our own response in the expressions of the men seated around the table, and then we see Jesus—at least Garibay's version—and we stop. Back up. Check the title of the painting to ensure we understood it correctly the first time: *Emmaus*. Garibay upends our expectations in this familiar scene by drawing the figure of Jesus as a laughing woman in a red café dress. In case we're uncertain, he includes the classic stigmata in her hands to reassure us that, yes, the artist intends for us to consider this woman to represent the resurrected Jesus. Garibay's delightful painting underscores how even when we are most fervently seeking God, we often miss God, who tends to show up in ways we never expected. This is the foundational tension in the plotline of Jesus living among a nation with specific expectations for their Messiah.

When God doesn't match our ideals or expectations, we are prone to miss the presence of God-with-us in the reality of our lives. Sometimes we don't see God because we are looking for something else—like me running around a monastery for a spiritual experience in a religious icon chapel and almost missing the presence of God quietly waiting for me in the beautiful flower garden. Sometimes, people who encounter God—even those of us who would consider ourselves seekers of God—do not find God because, in our disappointment with the outcomes of our lives, we've covered our vulnerable, seeking hearts in layers of self-protective cynicism. Cynicism and seeking repel each other and we lose the sense of God's real presence.

Sometimes we don't find God because we don't ever get close enough to the people God promises to be most present to. If anyone embodied the spirit of Emmanuel Garibay's *Emmaus*, it was the disruptive saint Dorothy Day. In her work to welcome the stranger and feed the poor, she cast a vision of communion, revealing the presence of God for all of us, writing in *The Reckless Way of Love*, "We cannot love God unless we love each other, and to love, we must know each other. We know Him in the breaking of bread, and we know each other in the breaking of bread, and we are not alone anymore. Heaven is a banquet and life is a banquet, too, even with a crust, where there is Companionship."[8] We understand Dorothy Day to mean the liturgical breaking of bread in our church worship, but from her life feeding the hungry and serving the poor, we can imagine Day is referring to literal bread as well. My friend Christine loves to remind everyone she meets that if they want to find the presence of God, they need to go spend time among the poor and marginalized.[9]

A few years ago my friend Brendah Ndagire, who grew up in Uganda, described her perspective of the road to Emmaus as a tutorial for practicing resurrection with the "poor, the marginalized, the wanderers, and the hopeless in our communities."[10]

As Brendah began walking through her city with eyes trained for the unexpected presence of the resurrected Christ, she noticed that unlike the disciples walking toward Emmaus who were "speaking to each other about everything," the people around her—even, she said, "in an economically poor nation like Uganda"—were too distracted by social media and smartphones to speak with each other about much, let alone *everything*. Even Christians who shared close relationship barely scratched the surface of talking about everything together, she noticed. She asked, "How likely is it that we would be able to speak with the economically poor, socially marginalized, and hopeless in our communities?"

Brendah added that Jesus not only walked and talked with the disciples in Luke 24, but he also asked provocative questions. For example: "What are you discussing together as you walk along?" I've always interpreted Jesus' question as tongue-in-cheek. A kind of *gotcha*, setting his friends up to laugh at themselves when they finally realize it was Jesus asking them the question. As I listen to Brendah's perspective, I hear this question in a new way. The disciples are processing deep grief, possibly talking through their tears. It doesn't seem likely that Jesus—known for being "moved with compassion"[11] when he encounters people in grief—would be playing a trick on them. In Brendah's interpretation, Jesus is modeling a way of engaging others by "asking questions and seeking understanding from those we encounter on the way."[12] Alongside the wisdom of Dorothy Day and my friend Christine, Brendah's words remind us that when we love anyone—especially the "overlooked or ignored" (Matthew 25:37–40, *The Message*)—in Jesus' name, Jesus tells us we are loving God, and in that way, mysteriously, we actually are able to find God.

None of those reasons—idealism, cynicism, or ignoring the presence of God at the communion table or among the poor—seem to be what keeps the Emmaus travelers from recognizing Jesus. Luke tells us that their eyes "were kept from recognizing him." We're given many reasons for this kind of blindness when it happens elsewhere in Scripture, including judgment for rebellious, hardened hearts who *refuse* to see (Isaiah 6:9; Isaiah 6:10; John 12:40; Acts 28:26; Acts 28:27; Romans 11:8). But something else seems to be happening here. Perhaps deep grief dulls their senses or perhaps in some way Jesus wants to reveal himself slowly out of love for them, but the Emmaus travelers aren't willfully refusing to see God. Though they admit despair—"but we had hoped"—they eventually recognize Jesus and declare that he is the Son of God, the Messiah. Why would God choose to keep them from recognizing Jesus immediately? Why not give them more moments to bask in his miraculous reappearance?

I don't know why, but I know that it's not because God is cruel, manipulative, or spiteful. There's another power at work here, and the practice of a Rule of Life has helped me to understand a paradox: seeking God is not a path I initiate but instead a path on which I place myself to be found by God. Seeking God and being found by God is not a means to an end, a point of arrival, but a way of being with God in a relationship. Seeking love and being found by love is the way the Holy Spirit initiates and continues to invite us into a friendship rather than a transactional relationship with God. I like to think about this habit of God's the way I once heard a monk describe in a story about an Irish nun who was fond of playing hide and seek with the "wee ones" in her care. When it was her turn to hide, she told friends with a twinkle in her eye, "I always try to let a part of myself stick out."[13]

While the Holy Spirit invites us to know God in the rhythms of seeking, finding, and being found, it's important to say that God's unexpected ways of being present to us don't always *feel* loving. The reality of God's initiating role and our responsive role means that it can at times feel like God is absent more than present and that we are helpless to do anything about it. I'll share some of those experiences from my life in the coming chapters, but I'm guessing you can easily recall times from your life when it felt like God might have been leaving all the work of seeking and finding to you. You might even feel that loss of sensing God's presence right now and are reading this book to find something—*anything*—that might help you find God again. It might feel like small comfort amid that kind of pain, but the truth is that even our awareness of God's absence is a reminder of God's real presence. Thomas Merton, yet another monk, says it this way: "We could not seek God unless He was seeking us. We may begin to seek Him in desolation, feeling nothing but His absence. But the mere fact that we seek Him proves that we have already found Him."[14] Even when God's presence feels like absence, it's rooted and grounded in the love we have, or once felt we had, in our relationship with Jesus.

ONE PATH: A RULE FOR HOLDING TOGETHER SEEKING AND BEING FOUND BY GOD

Paying attention to the present

How can a Rule of Life help us practice openness to mystery and train our eyes to notice all the ways God arrives in the reality, not idealized versions, of our lives?

The answer, for me, is one moment at a time, and one encounter at a time.

Even though they are often more famous for what they couldn't initially perceive, the Emmaus disciples can teach us a lot about seeking and finding God. As they return home from Jerusalem, sad and befuddled, they choose to walk and talk together. When given the opportunity to invite a stranger into their conversation, they share their story, not holding back even their sad emotions. They are listening closely enough to what the stranger has to say that they invite him home for dinner. Later, after their eyes are opened to the presence of Jesus, they will recall that their hearts were "burning within them" (Luke 24:32) as they listened to him explain the scriptures. But that's not even the end of what the Emmaus friends have to teach us. Luke 24 tells us that they immediately—"in the same hour" (Luke 24:33 NRSVue)—return to Jerusalem to tell Jesus' followers what they have seen and heard. This whole encounter is a rich example for us to follow as we enter a Rule of Life as a spacious path between Jesus, others, and our own hearts.

A Rule of Life helps us navigate our days between the concrete and the intangible places we hope to find God's presence.

The Emmaus disciples model several actions that we can practice in our everyday lives—disciplines that will help us discern those burning-heart moments as invitations to keep company with Jesus and train our instincts to respond and to share that invitation with others. Whether I'm practicing the traditional disciplines of the Christian life—scripture, church, and prayer—or engaging in less traditional practices, like reading poetry, walking around the block with my neighbor, or mopping the bathroom floor, I'm listening for the invitations of Jesus and training my senses to notice hints of his resurrected, loving presence. This practice goes with me in everything I do: walking to the mailbox, making small talk after church, lighting candles at the dinner table, selecting vegetables from the farmers market or the produce aisle, offering some change to the person asking for money at the stoplight, toasting my friends on their birthdays, swapping yard work with the neighbors, letting someone hug me when I'm really sad or mad, and countless other quotidian things. Anywhere I notice a flicker of life and love, I look for the presence of Jesus. So many times when I have asked the Holy Spirit where God was when I needed God most, it's these small, unexpected moments and the people with me in those moments that come to mind.

As I have continued to practice a Rule of Life, I've reexamined that beautiful paradox I found at the start: when we seek God, we discover that—through the invitations of Jesus—God's love sought and found us first. The circuitous journey of the spacious path faces us both inward—toward the inner circle of our own being, which is made beloved in God's image—and outward to share our belovedness with others, friends and strangers alike. In the next chapter, we'll explore five specific invitations Jesus gives us to follow his restful way in a fragmented world and what it might look like to respond to those invitations in a Rule of Life.

Let's begin with an honest assessment of our current reality. This is always a healthy place to start and worth spending a few minutes to put into words. We're all living by at least an *unwritten* rule of life—the default habits and practices that make up our movements from the time we wake up in the morning to the time we go to bed at night, and even as we sleep. We all navigate our days around profoundly embedded habits and beliefs about who we are and who we hope to be. Being able to notice your daily actions and habits with gentle curiosity instead of reflexive judgment is a good practice that will help you practice a Rule of Life as a spacious path.

What daily habits and rhythms are already part of your life? Be specific. Avoid a gut response to these questions by recalling what actually happens throughout your day instead of recording what should have happened or what you hoped would happen.

For the next twenty-four hours, become a student of yourself. Notice the following habits and practices with gentle curiosity toward yourself rather than reflexive judgment:

- How do you wake up? What gets you out of bed? What are you thinking and feeling?
- What are you doing first in the day? What are you doing last?
- Look at the other natural transitions from day to night, morning to afternoon. How do those transitions feel? What do you do in response to those natural transitions?

As you become aware of your daily habits and patterns, begin to name the emotions you feel in response to the noticing:

- Do your daily habits represent recent changes in the normal rhythms of your life? If so, how do you feel about those recent changes? If you're hoping to find a *new normal* in a season of change, what habits or patterns are you longing for?
- Alternatively, you might notice that your daily habits and patterns feel familiar, or maybe even overly familiar. You might feel stuck and in need of some changes. If so, how does that feel? Could you begin to name the changes you desire?

As you become aware of how you feel about daily habits and patterns, take some time to name the gifts, needs, desires, and losses your daily habits represent. Next, ask Jesus to give you the capacity to rejoice in the gifts and lament the losses. Lastly, ask Jesus to help you give voice to what you need and desire. From your reflection, complete this sentence as a prayer: "Jesus, as I consider a Rule of Life, I desire _____ and I need you to _____. Amen."

PART 1

*Saying Yes to the Rule of Life
as a Spacious Path*

*A rule that makes space to say yes to Jesus' invitations to
unforced rhythms of freedom and commitment*

Prepare for Part 1 by reading Matthew 11:28–30 and Luke
10:25–28.

Practicing a Rule of Life as a response to Jesus' invitation
for rest is a bit like my encounter with the prayer labyrinth
in Texas—a spacious pathway that, instead of disorienting or
trapping me, *reoriented* me in the direction of Jesus, others,
and myself. In her book *Seeking God: The Way of Benedict*,
Esther de Waal describes the Rule of Life as "taking us by the
hand and leading us to Christ."[1] Not only are we walking a
spacious path "earthed in Christ," and a Rule leading us to
Christ, but a Rule is also tuning our ears to the invitations of
Christ. Picking up the story of Benedict where we left off in
the introduction, we can imagine ourselves standing with his
friends at the mouth of the cave waiting to finally hear what
God has told him during all those years of solitude.[2] And the

first word he speaks is not a tested method for hearing God, but an invitation into a spiritual discipline, "Listen!" Following Benedict's lead, we begin a Rule of Life in the same way: we listen.

A Rule of Life makes space for us to say yes to all that Jesus invites and all that God commands. Jesus invites us to learn his "unforced rhythms of grace," which is a much different offer than any system for spiritual growth that we could initiate. A Rule helps us discern the practices and habits that Jesus is inviting, practically respond to those invitations in every part of our lives, and document the invitations in a meaningful way that will help us keep coming back to Jesus for rest.

A Rule of Life is a spacious path that helps us live our daily lives in the rhythms of Jesus. Visualizing the geometry of a prayer labyrinth helps me imagine the formational characteristics of practicing a Rule of Life. Whether you are building a Chartres-style labyrinth in your backyard or drawing it on a piece of paper, you'd begin with one vertical line intersected by one horizontal line—a cross. Next, you'd place a dot in each of the four quadrants and begin connecting the dots using the four points of the cross and four points of the quadrants. The person walking a labyrinth isn't aware of this structure because they are just stepping one foot in front of the other on the path. But if they could see themselves from above, they'd see that they are walking circuit after circuit through a cross-shaped quadrant—round and round the center of the labyrinth.

Medieval Christians adapted the labyrinth architecture to a four-fold symmetry for the obvious visual reason, but I think the benefit is more than visual. It's a way of embodying a spiritual reality that the path of resurrection life is formed in a crucifixion landscape. When Jesus invites us to the unforced rhythms of grace, he is inviting us to arrange our practices and habits in the same way he arranged his own—in the cruciform pattern of God's kingdom, where the cross is the path to resurrection. As we follow the restful way of Jesus, we pace our steps to these rhythms of commitment and freedom, where yokes become easy and burdens become light. The best part of this arrangement is that Jesus always wraps his invitations in God's love and God's faithfulness to accomplish all that God has given us to do through the Holy Spirit. (Philippians 1:6) This is what we mean by making space to say yes to all that Jesus invites and all that God commands.

In the prologue, we learned that the Rule of Life is a practice that helps us not only to seek God, but to make space for ourselves to be found by God. In the coming chapters, we'll consider how a Rule of Life helps us practice the rhythms of listening and responding to Jesus' invitations to come to him for rest in every part of our lives. We'll explore the Benedictine vows as a model for a Rule that helps us freely keep our commitments and discover how Benedict's twofold call to contemplation and community provides structure for the spacious path of a Rule of Life. Along the way, I'll share some examples of how practices of prayerful listening and loving presence have helped me say yes to a Rule of Life.

But first, I want to tell you about learning to dance.

CHAPTER 1

COME TO ME

*Saying Yes to Jesus' Invitation
to Unforced Rhythms of Grace*

I believe that we learn by practice. Whether it means to learn to
dance by practicing dancing or to learn to live by practicing living,
the principles are the same.

—MARTHA GRAHAM[1]

We live by rhythms. The earth spins in the rhythms of light
and energy, and our bodies pulse in rhythms of blood
and oxygen. In *The Message* version of Matthew 11, Jesus
describes his way of moving through the world as "unforced
rhythms of grace." Because rhythms make the world go round,
we emotionally perceive and physically sense, not just intellectually understand, the difference between forced and unforced
rhythms. Unforced rhythms work into the organic movements
we were born into and fit in with an instinctive awareness of
wholeness and well-being. Forced rhythms require an inordi-
nate amount of energy to maintain, yet it's possible to become
accustomed to their artificial and manufactured movements,
even as those movements exhaust us. Both kinds of rhythms
require practice, but only one nurtures life and rest. When we

discern a Rule of Life in the restful way of Jesus, we'll notice sensations of quietness, peace, and release of tension as indications that we are hearing the Holy Spirit and not merely our own initiative or someone else's agenda. In this way, restful rhythms become the rule by which we measure every part of a Rule of Life.

WE DIDN'T KNOW WE COULD DANCE

My husband and I didn't dance at our wedding. Even if it would have been permitted, we wouldn't have known how. We didn't drink then, either. It took ten years of keeping vows—some years, just barely—before we figured out we really needed to dance. We celebrated our tenth anniversary on a free Caribbean cruise and headed straight to the dance floor and the frozen fruity drinks. We closed the club each night, dancing off our pent-up piety.

Who told us we weren't supposed to dance?

To answer that question, I need to tell you about my grandparents. All through my childhood I had never seen them dance. One year, when I was well into my thirties, a few dozen extended family members gathered for Thanksgiving dinner at the local fire hall. After the meal, while we awkwardly tried to reconnect with cousins and uncles, an ambitious relative turned on some music and cleared the far side of the room to use as a dance floor. One by one a few cousins, especially the littlest ones, then an uncle and an aunt, began to twist and spin. Without much coaxing, Grandpa and Grandma took their turn on the floor. Cheered on by four generations of their family, they danced a perfect, playful foxtrot. Standing along the wall, my mother whispered to me, "All these years, they thought they weren't supposed to dance."

In a sincere attempt to follow Jesus, my grandparents compartmentalized their lives into spiritual and secular categories; dancing belonged in the latter. Thankfully, by the time my younger siblings were getting married, we began to dance at family weddings. At every reception, my grandparents foxtrotted into the middle of the floor, winning all the longest-married-couple contests.

How many times do we live like my grandparents thought they were supposed to live, understanding the freedoms and commitments Jesus invites us to live as systems to follow (or reject) rather than rhythms to keep? Like dance—at least the steps my grandparents learned—seeking God and being found by God relies on a rhythm of leading and following, which is a relational rhythm nurtured by trust and practice. Following is hard and practice takes time, and so, throughout history, humans have attempted to simplify the process by forcing spiritual formation into ill-fitting systems to prove spiritual maturity. This is not the restful way of Jesus—and not because Jesus shied away from rules or from freedom. In dance terms, Jesus both leads and follows; he holds the tension together in himself, as both God and human. Through his life of perfect obedience to God and through his perfect representation of God's love to us, we learn how to hold together both freedom and commitment.

LEARN THE UNFORCED RHYTHMS OF GRACE

Jesus invites us to follow his lead in the most unexpected terms: *Are you exhausted? Of course, you are; I can tell just by looking at you! Come over here by me and rest. Here, let me show you how. First, take this heavy farm implement. Got it? Now put it over your shoulders. No, not like that. Here, watch how I do it. Okay, now walk with me. There you go.*

Steady now. Keep time with me—lift and step, step, slow, slow, breathe [he adjusts the yoke]. Okay, begin again: lift, step, step, slow . . .[2] As an exercise of my imagination, this invitation doesn't make a lot of sense, but neither did the way I used to imagine this passage, as if Jesus were inviting me to pull up a lounge chair by the pool for a few hours.

During all those years of frustration, burning myself out on every endeavor of spiritual formation, I would read this passage and think: "Well, that's very nice of you, Jesus, but you know I don't have time for that! And, in case you've forgotten, let me remind you in full detail all the reasons I can't just sit down and rest with you: [insert long list of responsibilities overwhelming my life at that time]." If I'd been able to put it in words, I might have admitted that, instead of feeling invited, I felt like Jesus might have been taunting me, especially during the season when I was caring for four children under the age of six. Are you tired? Are you kidding me?! What I never noticed is that Jesus isn't describing a *sit down and put your feet up* kind of rest at all.

There's nothing wrong with that kind of rest, and throughout Scripture, we're invited to enjoy the physical refreshment that comes from leisurely rest. But what Jesus is inviting in Matthew 11 surpasses a long nap or a lazy day at the beach. He's offering a rest so deep we can experience it even as we work. A kind of rest that reaches into the most bone-crushing weariness of our souls, the place we're so tired we can't even pray, where we feel like no one else could possibly help us lighten the load of our lives. When I finally heard this scripture as an invitation, I responded wholeheartedly. I knew that kind of exhaustion, and, thought, oh yes, Jesus, I want to take you up on that offer. My goal in life became to answer the question: How does one do that? How do I live my everyday life in the reality of the rest Jesus is offering? What does it look like in the most practical ways to rely on Jesus to do the heavy lifting in the responsibilities I believe I'm supposed to be carrying?

To help us keep company with Jesus, whose idea of work and productivity is wholly different from our own, a Rule of Life subverts systems for accomplishment, spiritual or otherwise. Practicing a Rule of Life on the spacious path is like practicing the steps of a beautiful choreography where—following Jesus' lead—we find the movement of our lives hidden with his in the restful, loving presence of God. We can only love God because God first loved us; we can only seek and find God because God sought and found us first. This is the order of our relationship—God leads, and we follow, but not in a static, systematic way. Instead, in the movements of the Spirit of God that lives within us, our steps grow closer together, like the gracefulness of well-practiced choreography. In dance as in a Rule of Life, a partnership of trusted leading and following turns clunky stutter steps into joyful, fluid motion.

FIVE INVITATIONS: A RULE FOR HOLDING TOGETHER FREEDOM AND COMMITMENT

Listening and responding to Jesus' invitation to rest

How can a Rule of Life help us practice saying yes to the unforced rhythms of grace that Jesus invites us to walk with him? How can we understand the invitation to freely keep our commitments to Jesus as a rhythm to keep rather than a system to reject or follow? How in the world can practicing something as structured as a Rule of Life help us say yes when Jesus invites us to rest?

For several decades, including the years of moves and transitions and constant disorientation I describe in the introduction, I lived in a vicious cycle of trying to find the right productivity method to make my life work. As a student, then as a parent, and in various jobs and other professional pursuits, I felt I needed just the right to-do list that would guarantee outcomes and provide a sense of expertise and accomplishment. I applied the same method to every area of my life, including my relational and spiritual life. With this as my frame of reference, a Rule of Life became another system I hoped would produce my desired outcomes. Because I'd lived most of my life operating outside of the invitation to work alongside Jesus, I'd burned myself out after every endeavor. My default posture was *all or nothing*. This led to avoiding anything that looked or felt like a to-do-list for productivity for almost a decade.

As I began to see Matthew 11:28–30 as a profound invitation from Jesus, I recognized that I wasn't responsible to initiate my own plans for spiritual growth. I was only responsible to come to Jesus, who was already at work with purposes for my life, before I even *began* trying to master my own goals and desires. The passage helped me reimagine my role in that work as one who works alongside Jesus, watching and learning from him how to live as my truest self, the person God imagined from the beginning.

Most of us don't actively ignore the ideas and actions we suspect are coming from God, but plenty of us are tempted to believe we're responsible for outcomes in certain parts of our life—the parts we suspect God doesn't care about. This leaves us feeling like our lives are broken up into two compartments: the stuff Jesus oversees and the stuff we oversee. When we talk about feeling fragmented or scattered, sometimes this is the reason. Inadvertently, we've divided our lives into sections that we believe we're responsible to manage.

If life is a journey, then ours might feel more like a critter scurrying in a maze than a pilgrim walking a spacious path.

This is where the spiritual practice of a Rule of Life became most helpful to me. In writing his Rule, Benedict invited his community to step into—rather than away from—a daily tension between freedom and commitment. In monastic language, commitments are known as vows, and Benedictine monks still take the three vows written in the sixth-century rule: obedience, stability, and fidelity to the monastic way of life. Monastic vows were "total and consuming," according to Esther de Waal, but they paradoxically oriented the community in a freedom-loving way of life held together by "the need not to run away, the need to be open to change, the need to listen." According to her, the paradox is that these all-consuming commitments "bring freedom, true freedom."[3] Even in the most formal of religious commitments, the core desire for the Rule was simply to live in rhythms that helped monastic communities to seek God.

While they look different outside a monastery, the Benedictine vows offer a model for a Rule of Life that helps us say yes to all that Jesus invites and all that God commands. Throughout the book, we'll consider these commitments through the lens of five invitations Jesus gives in Matthew 11:28–30: Come to me, take my yoke, walk with me, work with me, and keep company with me invites us to say yes to restful rhythms, obedience, stability and change in the church, prayerful work, and hospitality. In the invitation to come to him for rest, Jesus leaves no part of our life behind. And he begins with the improbable image, not unlike the cross he also tells us to carry: *Take my yoke upon you.*

While I love thinking about Jesus' words as invitations, living in unforced rhythms frees us to rethink our preconceptions about words like *obedience* and *commands*. Invitation sounds restful to me, but I quickly associate commands and obedience with failure—my own and others'. Let's dare to imagine that saying yes to all that God commands is the restful way of Jesus and that a Rule of Life is a spacious path for obedience.

CHAPTER 2

TAKE MY YOKE

Saying Yes to Spacious Obedience

Obedience is the thing, living in active response to the living God. The most important question we ask of this text is not, "What does this mean?" but "What can I obey?"

—EUGENE PETERSON[1]

So obedience is really about love.

—ESTHER DE WAAL[2]

Saying yes to Jesus' invitation to spacious obedience brings us to this paradox: committing to follow Jesus' lead frees us to be hidden with Christ in the restful, loving presence of God. We are free to obey all that God commands because Jesus fulfilled all the requirements of the law and has made a way for us to join him in spacious obedience to God.

THE LAW OF LOVE

One of the most meaningful sentences I've ever read about spacious obedience was written in crayon. A couple of decades ago, as an earnest and unfortunately sometimes uptight young mom, I was teaching our preschool-aged sons the Ten

Commandments. Because they couldn't yet read and write, I'd given them each a three-ring notebook to draw their responses to our Bible lessons. On one page, under the very serious heading I had written— "Love the Lord God and don't put any gods before him"—our younger son, Alex, drew his response to the first commandment—a drawing that looked like any three-year-old's etching, including a large, semi-round circle signifying a head with three smaller, semi-round blobs signifying eyes and a nose. In dark crayon, Alex added an upturned hash mark as a smile, two hash marks out of the side of the head for arms and two hash marks five times longer signifying legs jutting straight from the bottom of the head-blob. In Alex's picture, this is God. I can tell because it takes up most of the page. Balancing on one of God's stick arms is a smaller, semi-round circle attached to two leg sticks standing straight up in the air. When I asked my son to title his picture, he dictated: "Alex standing on his head on God's arm showing that he loves God." A few pages later, under the heading: "What Jesus Means to Alex," he dictated: "He loves me. He likes me." Years later, while cleaning out the attic, I found Alex's drawing at a time I really needed to be reminded that I don't need other small gods when this God lets us stand on our heads to show that we love Him.

In the theology of a three-year-old, how hard can it be to obey a God who loves us and likes us?

OBEDIENTIA

Obedience is an old-fashioned word that we might throw in the same column as *rule* or *vow*, but it might help to know that the word *obedience* is derived from the Latin *oboedire*, which shares its roots with *audire*, to hear. As Benedict opened his rule with one word "Listen!", we could also imagine him saying "Obey!" In the closing paragraph of the prologue,

Benedict, echoing the psalmist's passion for God's law, reminds us that love is the fuel that energizes obedience:

> We shall run
> On the path of God's commandments,
> our hearts overflowing
> With the inexpressible delight
> of love.[3]

The Benedictine way of life centered around daily prayer and scripture reading, and the communal relationship that bound the monks together in love rooted itself in a shared love for God's commandments. In the Matthew 11 invitation to obedience we hear echoes of both the beginning and end of Benedict's prologue: listen and love. Jesus invites us to learn from him a restful way of obedience.

SPACIOUS OBEDIENCE
What spacious obedience is and what spacious obedience is not

In the context of Matthew 11, we're obeying the One who is already shouldering the weight of our lives. We obey with our whole selves out of love and gratitude and, in our obedience, find ourselves at rest. Mimicking the metaphor of a yoke, we "bend our will toward the will of Christ and find we are not alone but working in collaboration with Jesus."[4] When we obey his invitation with our whole selves, we practice his restful way.

Saying yes to spacious obedience is not the same thing as unquestioning compliance with no room to ask God for clarity. Acts of obedience, discerned by listening and responding to Jesus, are not acts of forced submission but a "free, humble, loving surrender to the will of God."[5] When I am standing at the point of obedience to Jesus and not able to see how anything good will come from my surrender, I often pray: "Jesus, show me how obeying you in this will lead me to rest." I ask this question as sincerely as I'm able, not wanting to test Jesus, but to remain openly curious: *I want to say yes to you, but I'm afraid I'm hearing you wrong because what I think you're asking me to do doesn't seem like it could possibly lead me into rest.* I don't often perceive a specific answer to my question, and I often need a group of trusted friends to help me discern the voice of Jesus. Whether I hear a clear response or not, something about forming the prayer—especially in the presence of my community—shifts my heart toward love.

Saying yes to spacious obedience is not the same thing as submitting to abusive or overbearing power. Obedience is inherently vulnerable and too often manipulated by people with positions of authority against the already-vulnerable, which is why it means so much that Jesus is a gentle and lowly leader. Saying yes to spacious obedience is saying yes to discerning the difference between humble leaders like Jesus and leaders who distort the gentle, lowly character of Jesus.

This second point feels especially important in our current context when so much hidden abuse and manipulation is being revealed within the church and other institutions within our society. Like historic spiritual practices known as a rule, old agricultural methods might feel from another era, which means that the metaphor Jesus uses in Matthew 11 can get a bit lost in translation; we might read the words and feel no connection to them at all. Alternatively, because both words, *rule* and *yoke*, fit the language and metaphors used by Christians and colonizing authorities to systematically oppress other humans, some of us might read the words and feel strong resistance. To talk about *a Rule of Life that helps us carry the easy yoke* may evoke a way of life that is harsh and deadly.

In his book *Gentle and Lowly*, author Dane Ortlund describes the paradox of Jesus' yoke this way:

> [Jesus'] yoke is a nonyoke, and his burden is a nonburden. What helium does to a balloon, Jesus's yoke does to his followers. We are buoyed along in life by his endless gentleness and supremely accessible lowliness. He doesn't simply meet us at our place of need; he lives in our place of need.[6]

Framed within an invitation to rest, the yoke that Jesus wants to share with us is a different yoke than any method of labor we've experienced, or world systems can imagine. When we say yes to spacious obedience, we are taking him at his word that this invitation is to a way of life that is not harsh, heavy, ill-fitting, or exploitative.

Here's another paradox about obedience: when we pick up the "nonyoke" of Jesus, we release the yokes we've placed onto others. It's impossible to simultaneously carry a nonburden while expecting others to remain weighed down in burdensome systems. We discover in our obedience that for Jesus' invitation to rest to be something we carry freely and lightly, it can only be received when it's extended to all. What a relief, and what a gift to share this holy, equitable rest.

Practicing a Rule of Life as an invitation to spacious obedience makes room for us to reimagine all our lives as collaborative work with Jesus, who shoulders the weight of our commitments. We love God because God loved us and liked us first. We obey God because, first, Jesus obeyed the Father in all that God gave him to do. "This grounding in love remains the vital element," writes Esther de Waal, ". . . the willing obedience which says 'Yes' with our whole person to the infinite love of God . . ." Obedience is our grateful "yes" to practice the restful way of Jesus.

CHAPTER 3

SAFEGUARDING LOVE

All the paths of the LORD are steadfast love and faithfulness, for those who keep his covenant and his decrees.

—PSALM 25:10 (NRSVUE)

When asked which command in the Torah was the greatest, Jesus began his response by echoing the formative Hebrew prayer known as the Shema: "Hear O Israel, the Lord is our God, the Lord is one." The reality of our triune God existing in perfect communion with each other—unity in diversity—lays the foundation for every other relationship, the ground in which love is rooted. And it begins with the first word of the prayer, the word for which it is named—*shema*, which means "hear" or "listen."

Five centuries later, Benedict emerged from his cave echoing the same prayer: "Listen." Later in his prologue, Benedict describes the purpose of the Rule as a "little discipline to safeguard love." These two invitations of Benedict's rule—to listen and to safeguard love—crystallized during his years of practicing solitude. When Benedict gave himself to the work of listening, he understood that God was calling him into a life of humility expressed in two parts: contemplation (a life of prayer) and community (a life of love). In his teaching on *Crafting A Rule of Life*, Stephen Macchia encourages us to place emphasis in the phrase *Rule of Life* not on rule, but on life.[1] Likewise, with Saint Benedict's exhortation to "safeguard love," we could even consider calling the practice a Rule of Love. In Luke 10, Jesus offers an invitation to follow God's rule of love when he sums up all of God's law into what we've come to call the "greatest commandments."

WHAT IS WRITTEN IN THE LAW?

In Luke 10:25–28, we see Jesus listening to the heart of the law expert's question. The man thought he was asking for a list of behaviors that he hoped would determine his future in eternity, but Jesus—the embodied fulfillment of the Law— reframed the question in terms of love. All of this, he says—all the good works, smart talk, and rule-following—are nothing compared to love. Sadly, the law expert could not listen, as we go on to read. He remains fixated on his agenda. He wants to nitpick the rules for loving neighbors. In the face of love, the law expert chose rules. Love for rules is his burden, and it is a heavy one.

I'm not an expert in religious law, but the questions this man asks resonate with me. I read Jesus' words and sometimes still wonder, *What about all the other commandments?* What I'm questioning is not Jesus but myself: What would happen if I let go of all my little rules for living (or, for some of us free spirits, my rules for *not* living by rules)? By echoing the Shema in Luke 10, Jesus doesn't just distill the breadth and scope of God's law into two commandments; he also echoes the power- ful, unified simplicity of the love of the communal Father, Son, and Holy Spirit. Each of the commandments are important, but when Jesus tells us which is the greatest, he isn't telling us the rest don't matter: he is giving us fresh eyes to see all that God commands in the light of God's intentions, in Benedict's terms, to "safeguard love." The rest of the commandments find their rightful place as a law of love when we remember that Jesus' life, death, and resurrection perfectly fulfilled God's law and demonstrated God's love.

Like the desire to prove my significance in a completed to-do list, I know the temptation to live by a law of rules rather than a law of love. For a long time into my adulthood, I blamed this tendency on the conservative church rules of my childhood. As I've grown in understanding about my own tendencies toward love for rules instead of a rule for love, I've come to understand that this is not a problem unique to me, the law expert in Luke 10, or the conservative church of my childhood. The experience of learning the Bible as a rulebook in my formative years buried my instinct for a loving, childlike faith, it's true, but I've come to understand that legalistic religion was not solely to blame—rather that I'm human, prone to wander away from God and toward self-righteousness instead.

In fact, I've observed that of all the *-isms* fragmenting our society, legalism might be the one we hold most in common. I've noticed that humans, in general, no matter to which side of polarized ideologies we most lean, love creating strict codes for what is okay and what is not, who is in and who is out. (Even anarchists who would recommend we throw off all laws preach their viewpoint legalistically!) We love legalism, and, surprisingly, coming to this awareness has felt like a relief to me. In our shared brokenness that enforces a litigious code for love rather than God's law of love, I'm responding to Jesus' invitation to tenderly accept all of us. God bless us; we're only human. On our best days and with our best ideas, no one has given a better vision for a law of love than Jesus. Saying yes to a Rule of Life on the spacious path Jesus commands in Luke 10 frees me to practice a rule that safeguards rather than codifies love.

TWO BORDERS: A RULE FOR HOLDING TOGETHER LAW AND LOVE

How can practices of humble, prayerful listening and loving, embodied presence help us say yes to a Rule of Life? How can the structures of making commitments and obeying God's commands fit into a Rule of Life that's a spacious path?

Discerning with listening and love

Unlike a maze, a prayer labyrinth doesn't require us to solve the riddle of how to find the right path leading us to the middle; by remaining within the borders of the pathway, placing one foot in front of the other, we always arrive at the center. Through my first experience walking a prayer labyrinth, uncertain how each turn of the circuits could possibly be leading me to the innermost circle, it was the two borders of the pathway that kept me moving in the right direction.

In the spacious path of a Rule of Life, we are given two borders as well, a twofold calling that Benedict named contemplation (a life of listening) and community (a life of love), which together provide a structure to keep us moving toward the center of God's restful, loving presence. From our first moments on earth, we reach for a connection with other souls.[2] Yet individuality rather than community is the dominant narrative of our society. Catholic social worker Dorothy Day famously described the tension of individualism as the "long loneliness," a condition we have all experienced. She taught with her words and her life that the only solution for the long loneliness is "love that comes with community."[3]

The Rule of Life as a spiritual practice assumes that we live with and for others. Jesus makes that same assertion when he summarizes all the law and the prophets into the greatest commandments: love God and love your neighbor as yourself. Yet, in much of the current teaching about the spiritual practice of a Rule of Life, the role of community takes up much less ink than the role of the individual. While the practice itself is a living, breathing, dynamic discipline that keeps us connected with the ancient and forever community of Jesus—in prayer, hospitality, study, work, and rest—community is the context for how we discern a Rule of Life in the first place.

In my experience, this means I need to expand my discernment process from the confines of my personal calendar and journal reflections on my own spiritual, emotional, and physical experiences to the wider reflections of the global and historic church. Like viewing the night sky with a telescope instead of the naked eye, a Rule of Life places the beauty of my personal desires and duties into the brilliant constellation of God's family story.

Discernment doesn't flourish when we practice it alone. Discernment, like a Rule of Life, becomes a *spiritual* practice when it humbly invites the voices of others. There are at least two significant reasons why this is true. One, we are made in the image of a communal God—the same God who decided within the community of Father, Son, and Holy Spirit to create us, in the first place. And two, because we are not God, and our ability to know what's best in any given moment is severely limited by countless realities of living within finite bodies in a broken world.

We often associate discernment with the choices we make related to vocation and calling—questions like what kind of education do I need, should I live in this city, or take that job, or marry this person, or not get married at all? It's true, we need help with those decisions. But I want to focus more on the way discernment guides the ordinary, everyday matters included in a spacious Rule of Life—one that's sturdy enough to take with us whether our lives consist of constancy or change. More specifically, I'd like to invite you to imagine how the practices of humble, prayerful listening and loving, embodied presence not only help to discern a Rule of Life but become themselves the practices that make up a Rule of Life.

CONTEMPLATION AND COMMUNITY

In this universe we are given two gifts: the ability to love, and the ability to ask questions. Which are, at the same time, the fires that warm us and the fires that scorch us.

—MARY OLIVER[1]

Bordered by faithful practices of listening and love, the Rule of Life is a spacious path to live out all that Jesus invites in Matthew 11:28–30 and all that God commands, summed up in Jesus' words to the law expert in Luke 10:25–28. Contemplation and community not only help us discern, but also take comfort together that we are given everything we need to live like Jesus, who fulfilled all of God's requirements and holds together in himself perfect obedience to God's law and perfect representation of God's love. Jesus is the way of the spacious path, leading us to find ourselves hidden with him in God's restful, loving presence, and his way is so spacious it makes room for us to travel together.

Let's begin by zooming in on each border of the spacious path: contemplation (a life of listening) and community (a life of love) as practices of discernment.

CONTEMPLATION AS A LIFE OF HUMBLE, PRAYERFUL LISTENING

The story is told of Mother Teresa that when an interviewer asked her, "What do you say when you pray?" she answered, "I listen." The reporters paused a moment, then asked, "Then what does God say?" and she replied, "He listens." It is hard to imagine a more succinct way to get at the intimacy of contemplative prayer.

—MARILYN MCENTYRE[2]

We'll begin where Benedict began—with contemplation, which I'm defining broadly as humble, prayerful listening. Because contemplation nurtures intimacy with God and intimacy often feels uncomfortable, contemplation can fail to move from an ideal to real practice, leaving us to feel like, somehow, we don't have what it takes to be contemplative people. While contemplation trains our physical selves to perceive spiritual realities, the practice is not a mystical ritual for the spiritually elite. Throughout scripture we observe a variety of ways God's people approach God in prayer, and even more ways that God approaches people. Because Jesus has reconciled us to God, we are welcomed into God's presence just as we are, in our real and present state.

When I first became aware of the spiritual practice of contemplation, I spent so much time feeling uncertain that my little moments of silence and open-ended listening prayer were meaningful in any way. I'd turn off external noise, close my eyes, and, instead of feeling closer to God, just feel lost in my own random and mundane thoughts. The moments of quiet didn't seem to add up to anything particularly meaningful. I've learned that often that's what contemplation is supposed to feel like: a kind of surrender to silence with no agenda to get any profound feeling or insight out of it.

Around this time, we moved to a house within earshot of a church bell that chimed every fifteen minutes of the day. I loved the bell for its village charm but stopped noticing it soon after we moved into the neighborhood. As a baby step into the discipline of contemplation, I asked God to alert me to the sound of the bells each hour and committed that, in return, I would take those moments to pause, turn down the volume of my thoughts, breathe deeply, and listen. For what I wasn't sure, but I knew that was also part of the deal—this emptying of mental, emotional, and physical noise to sit with the present God. I'd love to tell you that the experiment with the church bells was an overwhelming success; as it happened, I only noticed them a couple of times within the first week. I was quickly frustrated, because it seemed like a lot of work to stop whatever I was doing mid-track and do instead what felt like nothing. My mind wandered toward counting the bell chimes, praying for someone else, or imagining something God wanted me to know.

I know I'm not alone in struggling to practice contemplation. Recently I was talking with a friend about the challenges it presents: What even is it, exactly? And why does it often feel so hard? Around the same time, I read this warning from Thomas Merton: "As soon as you think of yourself as teaching contemplation to others, you make another mistake. No one teaches contemplation except God, who gives it. The best you can do is write something that will serve as an occasion for someone else to realize what God wants of him."[3] Okay, then. Keep reading.

Contemplation as spacious trust

While acknowledging the challenge of teaching something that is ultimately a gift of God's presence, there are a few truths about this spiritual practice that can help us imagine how to remain open and attentive to God. Contemplative listening takes many forms, but the core elements of contemplative prayer remain essentially the same: silence or at least a willingness to become quiet, an awareness of your whole self—body, mind, and emotions in the present moment—and no agenda other than to be open to God's presence. Spiritual contemplation requires sitting, soaking, and allowing the Spirit of the present God to wash and rumble and erode our defense mechanisms into receptiveness. Humbly, we lower our guard and prayerfully listen in the company of Jesus.

For me, contemplative prayer most often begins in circumstances when I simply pause wherever I am—in solitude, in the company of trusted friends, or in the middle of a busy place—and direct my attention to God's unseen presence for a moment or two. In my spiritual direction training, we learned this pause in terms of the Hebrew word *selah* (see-lah). The word repeated throughout the Psalms is probably a musical reference, calling for a break in the singing of the psalm. The *Amplified Bible* expands the meaning of the word to "pause, and calmly think of that" each time *selah* shows up in the text.

So, as I enter a contemplative pause, I understand that there's no need to strive for profound spiritual insight or a solution to a problem. I desire only to be still. As I, inevitably, begin to sense thoughts or feelings bubbling up in the quiet, I notice them without trying to analyze them. As I become aware of myself in God's presence, I notice the exact places in my body that I feel distracted or tired or anxious—my clenched jaw and my hunched shoulders or the weird twitch in my right eye. I might find myself recalling a time God met me in a similar place before, and I might notice a little beat of hopeful emotion rise. I might feel gratitude or even whisper

"Thank you," or echo the psalmist: "Selah, pause and calmly think of that."

I might also notice words from scripture begin to float through my mind. If that feels helpful, I might even try taking some deep breaths and gently let the words float in and out with my breath. For example, if I've paused in a moment when anxiety is threatening to capsize my day, I might hear snatches of Philippians 4:6–7 flicker like a little light in the back of my mind. I might pace the rhythm of my breathing to those snatches of scripture: Peace (inhale) that passes understanding (exhale); peace (inhale) passes understanding (exhale). I might even find myself resting my head on the back of my chair, closing my eyes for a few minutes, and letting go of all the thoughts and sensations I've been noticing, trusting that as I stop trying to solve the riddle of whatever has prompted my nervous energy, that my focus will shift instead to Jesus who is keeping company with me. Then, at some point, an alarm will ring, or someone will enter the room, and I'll move back into my day. Maybe I'll feel restored or maybe I'll feel frustrated that I only had long enough to realize how tired I am. Whatever I notice as I return to my other work is worth noticing in the presence of God. Jesus is with me still.

COMMUNITY AS A LIFE OF LOVING, EMBODIED PRESENCE

"But it does not seem that I can trust anyone," said Frodo.

Sam looked at him unhappily. "It all depends on what you want," put in Merry. "You can trust us to stick with you through thick and thin—to the bitter end. And you can trust us to keep any secret of yours—closer than you keep it yourself. But you cannot trust us to let you face trouble alone, and go off without a word. We are your friends . . ."

— J. R. R. TOLKIEN[4]

A Rule of Life is an act of both communal discernment and individual agency. Benedict began from a place of isolation, alone in his cave, listening for God's direction, yes. But we're told that even then, he relied on friends to bring him food[5], and he gave time to local people who dropped by to ask him what he was hearing from God. After three years of listening on his own and with this ad hoc fellowship, Benedict emerged from the cave to call women and men to join him in listening and love. From the beginning, the Christian community is embedded in the very practice of both discerning a Rule of Life and living it out.

Community will be an important part of our overall Rule of Life, incorporated into our daily, weekly, and seasonal rhythms because community has always been an important part of spiritual life. We see this truth first in the communal Trinity. We see it from the garden where God and humans made space each day to be together, to the feast days of the Hebrew Old Testament—structured around the rhythms of community worship life—to the life Jesus lived with his followers, into the origins of the early church described in Acts 2:42 who "devoted themselves to the apostles' teaching, to the community, to their shared meals, and to their prayers" (CEB).

For some of us, the meaning of community will be formalized and expressed by one Rule written, like Benedict's, for an entire community. This could be in the traditional sense of a monastery or intentional community arrangement. But it can also be an expression of shared callings. Berkeley Divinity School at Yale, for example, offers a Rule of Life "to give substance and shape to the fulfillment of [the seminary's] ambitions, not by establishing an inflexible regula, but rather by describing a normative pattern."[6] As part of my ongoing engagement with the organization that trained me as a spiritual director, I commit to following a shared Rule of Life—a list of values that form us as a fellowship—to foster spiritual companionship with other spiritual directors. We commit to attending one retreat or conference a year to nurture and refine our calling as spiritual directors and to seeking regular care for our souls through spiritual direction and supervision.[7] Community and support groups come together around shared commitments, like the Twelve Steps used in Alcoholics Anonymous.

Whether written by an individual to include a community or by a community to gather individuals, a Rule of Life helps us embody the nature of the triune God in which we were created. As we receive the gift of God's presence, we share it with others. This is what it means to love God and to love our neighbors as ourselves.

Community as spacious trust

In terms of spiritual practices, embodied presence takes many forms, but the core elements of loving community remain essentially the same: rooted and grounded in the love of Jesus who reconciled us to the communal welcome of the triune God, we are freed to be reconciled with others and ourselves. Sounds simple, yet I've found—and likely so have you—that loving presence is the most vulnerable part of saying yes to Jesus' invitations. Discovering that we are found by a God who loved us first, we are freed to love others and ourselves with ordinary as well as radical acts of loving presence. Humbly, we lower our guard and, in the company of Jesus, welcome each other's presence.

During my spiritual direction training I was assigned a book[8] that helped me think through each of the stages of my developing faith as a timeline of my life since the time when

I began to follow Jesus. As I charted my journey of faith, I noticed some painful patterns in my relationships. Some were current experiences with loss and disillusionment, and some were from childhood, but, together, all of them told me something important. Sketched in pencil, I could plainly see that my relationships provided the largest influence, for good or for ill, in every stage of my faith journey.

This correlated with another prominent theme from my reading, which I euphemistically labeled "The Question of Trust." One of the reflection questions asked, "Do you see yourself as a predominantly trusting or untrusting person?" My answer: "There's definitely a paradox here!" What on earth does that mean? Maybe I meant to say *painful, leaking wound where my heart used to be,* but *paradox* took less time to write?

In the overview of my life, trust swings like an overwound pendulum. As I looked back one season at a time, I could see seasons when the trust pendulum swung full force one direction—bypassing a healthy, wholehearted belief in the best of people—and then kept on going to the trust-people-at-all-costs side. In another season, the trust pendulum swung in the opposite direction toward a healthy, but cautious, slow discernment before swinging wildly to the "there-are-two-people-in-the-world-I-trust-and-I'm-not-even-sure-about-them" side. When the pendulum gets stuck on the trust-at-all-costs side, I have lived out of an idealistic, romanticized, and boundaryless perspective of relationships. On the other extreme, I have operated out of a fearful, critical, hypervigilant suspicion of people and their motives. Neither extreme is a place of wholeness and openness.

I drew this "paradox" into my journal as an actual line, with the extremes labeled at each end, and then marked over the middle the words "Freedom to trust people appropriately." This sort of balance of the trust pendulum is weighted by the belief that the Holy Spirit instructs and nurtures my ability to give and receive trust. Jesus is the source of true wholeness, and will lead and protect through, and sometimes despite, my relationships with others.

The freedom to trust people appropriately is one of the best gifts I've received as community has helped me discern and practice a Rule of Life as a spacious path. As I keep company with Jesus, others, and my own self, I discover that God's loving presence is never depleted. Together, we can take comfort that we are given everything we need to live like Jesus, who fulfilled all of God's requirements and holds together in himself perfect obedience and perfect love. And as I return to the center of God's beloved community, I can give and receive love again and again.

THREE COMPANIONS: A RULE FOR HOLDING TOGETHER CONTEMPLATION AND COMMUNITY

Which comes first—contemplation or community to help us discern a Rule of Life? I humbly offer the answer I've found to be true for me: both/and. When it comes to answering the questions embedded in a Rule of Life—How can I find God? How can I learn to pray? Where in the world can I find rest? —I need all the help I can get.

Keeping company with Jesus, others, and myself

In saying yes to a Rule of Life, I've opened myself to listen prayerfully to a loving community to help me wait on God for answers to my deepest questions about God, myself, and the world around me. I'm also making space to regularly practice humble, prayerful listening to the Holy Spirit's invitations through scripture, silence, and my own soul. Surrounding ourselves with humble, prayerful listening and loving, embodied presence, we find the help we need to discern and practice a Rule of Life as a spacious path. In this company, we bring our full selves into the companionship of Jesus and others and, much like the proverb "A cord with three strands is not quickly broken," we learn how to be present to all three at once. In the restful way of Jesus, learning how to be present in the direction of Jesus, others, and ourselves at once takes time and practice—a lifetime, actually, of following Jesus' unforced rhythms of grace.

Throughout the book, my hope is that by describing some of my own experiences as well as those I've been able to witness within community, you'll be able to better imagine how contemplation and community will help you grow, not only in your own capacity for prayerful listening and loving presence, but also in recognizing others who could come alongside you in discerning a Rule of Life. The experiences and practices I describe orient us in all three directions of discernment:

Contemplation

1. Contemplation as prayerfully listening to God
2. Contemplation as prayerfully listening to others
3. Contemplation as prayerfully listening to ourselves

Community

1. Community as loving presence in communion
2. Community as loving presence with the vulnerable
3. Community as loving presence with family, friends, and neighbors

The borderlines on the spacious path of a Rule of Life are mapped out by acts of discernment practiced in humble, prayerful listening and loving, embodied presence with God, others, and our own souls. If I had to answer the question of where to start first—contemplation or community—I'd say start with a practice of communal contemplation. Start with spacious silence that makes room for prayerful listening and loving presence all at the same time.

How often do we sit together in silence? It's rare enough for us to sit in silence alone, even more when we are together! One of the reasons I love attending our church is that I can answer the question confidently. At least once a week, our congregation sits together for one to two minutes of silence. From his first sermons in Connecticut and in nearly every service over the past seven years, Brian and our other clergy members have invited us to sit in silence, often but not always at the close of the sermon.

I'm not sure our congregation knows it, but Brian's inspiration came not from his seminary class or a favored preacher but from an unassuming Fred Rogers during his 1997 televised acceptance speech for a Lifetime Achievement award. In a room full of people who make millions performing passionate speeches on cue, Mr. Rogers stood at the podium and invited the room of celebrities to sit together in silence. His entire speech took less than two minutes and less than two hundred words, and right in the middle, he said, "Would you just take along with me ten seconds to think of the people who have helped you become who you are—those who have cared about you and wanted what was best for you in life? Ten seconds of silence. I'll watch the time." He looks at his watch while the camera pans the audience of teary men and women following Mr. Rogers's lead.

So, every week, Brian says, "Will you take one minute to sit silently with God? You bow your head and close your eyes. I'll watch the time." And we do, and he does.

You might not be able to ask your entire congregation to sit in silence every week, but you can share this invitation to silence with your church community in whatever way is available to you. Of course, listening to God in silence does not mean we need to hear anything. We might enjoy what Mother Teresa described as just a kind of listening to each other with no one doing any talking. By keeping silence together, we understand that sometimes we're just holding space for our friends to hear something from God. Perhaps the most treasured gift of silence is the way that together we can be reminded with no words at all that God loves us and God likes us.

SAYING YES TO THE RULE OF LIFE AS A SPACIOUS PATH

Your word is a lamp to my feet and a light to my path.
—PSALM 119:105 (NRSVUE)

Read Matthew 11:28–30 slowly and, if possible, out loud a couple of times. What word or phrase catches your attention? How does your body feel as you read Jesus' invitation to come to him for rest? What questions come to mind? What do you need help with to say yes to Jesus' invitation? Could you put that need into a one-sentence prayer for help?

FOR FURTHER REFLECTION

1. How did the description of a walking a labyrinth through an invisible cross-pattern resonate with your understanding of what it means to walk a spacious path with Jesus? How might this sentence inform your practice of a Rule of Life: "It's a way of embodying a spiritual reality that the path of resurrection life is formed in a crucifixion landscape"?

2. At first glance and without analyzing your answers, which of the five invitations in Matthew 11:28-30 (described in chapter 1) are you most drawn to? Which are you least drawn to?

3. From what you've read in chapter 2, what sounds inviting to you about spacious obedience? What sounds hard?

4. Chapter 3, "Safeguarding Love," invites us to consider the tension between exploring the freedom of God's love with the desire to follow God's laws. How have you experienced a connection between love and obedience? How would you restate Benedict's phrase "a little discipline to safeguard love" in your own words?

5. As you read the descriptions of contemplation and community in chapter 4, what feels inviting to you in your life right now? What feels incompatible with your life right now?

6. Where in your life are you connected to a community who actively listens to and restfully responds to what Jesus invites and commands? How could you invite this community to come alongside you as you discern a Rule of Life?

7. As you continue to notice the everyday pattern of your life with gentle curiosity rather than reflexive judgment, what experiences or practices from this section feel most inviting to your Rule of Life? Share your response with a trusted friend. Ask them to simply pray for you.

FURTHER PRACTICES FOR CONTEMPLATION AND COMMUNITY: *LECTIO DIVINA* AND SPIRITUAL DIRECTION

One of the best ways to start cultivating the skill of contemplative listening is by prayerfully reading and listening to scripture. I've found that as I draw near to God's word in listening prayer, I am moved to invite others to join me there. Sometimes I do this in more formal practices of spiritual direction groups; other times it's more informal, welcoming others to join me in listening to God and expressing God's love. Here are two practices that have become essential to discerning and practicing a Rule of Life.

SCRIPTURE

Benedict organized his rule around a communal life of contemplating—not merely studying but living with—scripture. Monks spent hours, individually and together, praying, singing, and reading scripture. They also set aside time for personal Bible reading and memorization. Since most of us reading this book do not live in a monastic community, how might we arrange our lives around listening to scripture? Perhaps the most important step we can take is to root ourselves in the love of Christ and in a community who listens to Jesus' invitations and loves God's commandments. Many of us learn early on in our Christian formation to read, study, and memorize the Bible. Most of us also learn that one of the primary ways to encounter scripture is to listen to a preacher or teacher exegete passages—to help us understand the layers of truth God has given us in the Word. In my experience, it's much rarer to hear encouragement to listen to scripture with no agenda, to release our need to know in a cerebral way to make space to perceive scripture with our whole person—body, heart, and mind.

Lectio divina or "sacred reading" is a method of reading scripture that's been used by the church for centuries. It incorporates several ways of interacting—intellectually, emotionally, and physically—with God through scripture into one practice. The four steps used in lectio divina might feel a bit cumbersome at first but will eventually become a natural way to be present to God as we read scripture.

Four Steps of Lectio Divina

1. Read (*lectio*)
Slowly and gently read and reread a passage of Scripture until a word or phrase draws your attention. Notice any strong emotion that comes as you consider the word or phrase.

2. Meditate (*meditatio*)
Once you have landed on a word or phrase, gently repeat it to yourself. Receive and reflect on the thoughts, hopes, images, and feelings that come to you through this word or phrase. Ask yourself: What is being offered to me through this scripture?

3. Pray (*oratio*)
Allow your whole being to become prayer. Honestly express your deepest thoughts, feelings, and desires in dialogue with God. Pray this way until you feel your energy shift to a sense of being "emptied out."

4. Rest (*contemplatio*)
Gently let go of all thoughts and feelings. Drop into God's presence beneath your thoughts and feelings. Just be in God's presence. Rest completely in God, grateful for what has been given. End your time with a simple chorus or prayer of thanks.

There are many methods for listening to scripture contemplatively, but the basic elements to humbly and prayerfully listening to scripture and the Holy Spirit are the same no matter which we choose. The reward is that we grow in our capacity to offer humble, prayerful listening in all our relationships. Either way, my capacity to hold space for God, others, and myself grows in the restful way of Jesus, who is the Word of God.

SPIRITUAL DIRECTION

Spiritual direction is a practice for those who wish to grow in their capacity to recognize God's voice and movement in the whole of their lives. By inviting a trusted and often trained companion to listen to the questions, prayers, and practices of my life, I better notice the Holy Spirit's invitations to keep company with Jesus, others, and my own soul. A spiritual director is someone who will listen, discern, pray, and rest with me in the presence of the triune God. To be fully observant of the movements of God in my life, a spiritual director also listens and tends to their own soul in the care of others.

Whether one-on-one or in a group format, spiritual direction is a beneficial co-practice to a Rule of Life, creating a steady, spacious place for us to practice listening and responding to the Holy Spirit's invitations. In the company of the triune God and a spiritual director or spiritual direction group, I discern fruitful practices to include in a Rule of Life. Most importantly, spiritual direction helps us remember that we are God's beloved child, welcomed into the companionship of Father, Son, and Holy Spirit and refreshed to share that welcome with others.

If you don't know where to find a trained spiritual director, here are a couple of helpful resources:

- Directory of spiritual directors trained through Selah: Leadership Transformations: https://www.leadershiptransformations.org/directory-of-spiritual-directors/
- Directory of ESDA's network of spiritual directors: https://www.graftedlife.org/spiritual-direction/find

PART 2

*Centering a Rule of Life
on the Spacious Path*

*A rule that makes space for my true self within the beloved,
baptized community of the triune God*

Prepare for Part 2 by reading Mark 1:9–11 and Matthew
17:1–8.

A Rule of Life makes space for us to walk together within
the diversity of God's beloved community. Centering a
Rule in the baptized, beloved community of God makes room
for us to ask the profoundly human questions of identity: Who
am I? How has God imagined me to live? In the company of
Jesus and in the communion of the saints, we begin where
Saint Benedict began. We listen!

A Rule of Life makes a spacious path for the incredible
reality that we are the *imago Dei*, created in the image of the
triune God, invited into the unity in diversity of God's beloved
community. Many methods for spiritual growth focus on our
individuality. While we are one important part of a whole, discerning a Rule of Life from an individual perspective is not a

spacious or restful way to follow Jesus. We are called to travel together following one triune God who offers one baptism into one body of Christ yet is made up of many parts.

Not only are we one of a whole, but we are invited to bring every part of ourselves into loving communion. Within our one whole self, we are (at least) three parts: body, mind, and emotions. Many programs and practices speak to one part of ourselves—exercise regimens, Bible reading plans, academic curricula, and professional ladders for promotion all exist to give us direction for highly-focused tracks for personal growth. A Rule of Life is a wider lens that takes in our inestimable worth as fully formed human beings made in the image of a wholly good and creative God. Implicit to this perspective is that there is a true, or authentic, identity imprinted on us by our Creator, who imagined all of the best ways to display the image of God in all people.

We've considered the invitation to say yes to a Rule of Life as spacious path to seek God and discover that we have already been found by God. Next, we'll fix our eyes on the heart of a Rule of Life, centering our identity as one of God's beloved. It helps me to imagine the center of a prayer labyrinth—the inner part encircled by the pathway. Like our truest self, hidden with Christ in God, the center is home base, the place that draws us inward and moves us outward, the place we arrive again and again.

We'll listen for and respond to the invitation to center a Rule of Life in the belovedness of God's unity in diversity, and nurture intimacy with God and loving communion with others. As we begin the practice of a Rule of Life, hidden in God with the beloved Christ, we'll also explore how a Rule of Life helps us to recognize and share that belovedness with others. Along the way, I'll offer examples of how practices of prayerful listening and loving presence have helped me center a Rule of Life within Christ's beloved church.

First, I want to tell you about the community that shaped my default rule of life for church.

CHAPTER 5

WALK WITH ME

*Saying Yes to Spacious Stability and
Change in the Church*

Church, with all its imperfections, is faith's incubator. Church is
faith's hospital and its picnic grounds, its sheltering tree and also
the rich soil from which it grows. Church embraces faith and holds
it tenderly with strong arms. It embraces me. And so I love the
church, even when it expects more of me than I think it should.

—KAREN STILLER[1]

Making a commitment to embrace stability and change in
a community sounds hard enough for monks, and—in
a world where unprecedented numbers of people are questioning the need for the church at all—it's even harder to
imagine making a similar commitment to our local church.
Yet, held in tension, the invitations to spacious stability and
change develop the freedom to live as what some might call
a non-anxious presence in worship. It helps to examine our
introduction to church and to consider how our early experiences form our expectations and longings for a spiritual home.

GOING TO CHURCH IN MY PARENTS' LIVING ROOM

In 1977, my father quit his job as a pastor to take up pastoring for free. He'd been working as a youth pastor for the church where he grew up, but when he began making radical suggestions for the church to reach out beyond its walls, the deacons asked him to be a visitation pastor instead. In the old days, visitation pastors were the ones in charge of visiting the sick and homebound church members and anyone who might be too ashamed to sit with rest of the congregation on Sunday mornings.

My dad would have been a good visitation pastor if it weren't for the neighbors filling up our living room for Bible study each week. They were asking the same uncomfortable questions as my father, and so we became a house church before that was trendy. Church in my earliest memories is vibrant, if not a bit chaotic, and easy to think of in terms of Jesus's invitation to walk with him as a member of a church community. Yet parts of my experience as a pastor's daughter left me with a limp, causing me to hobble into each church community I've entered since 1977.

The church of my childhood gathered as a small expression of sweeping reform in an established denomination, and so I learned to long for a church community open to change when old ways of worship form us apart from Jesus' ways. At the same time, my parents and five siblings literally relied on our small church to remain stable enough to pay for our grocery and heating bills, and so I learned at a visceral level that a church that feels unstable threatens my human need for security. As a result, my early experiences with church have informed all that I'm anxious about and all that I've been longing for ever since.

STABILITAS

Stabilitas (stability) means to make a vow to a life of fidelity to the monastic order. We could think of it in simpler terms as a promise monks make to not to run away when things get hard. For those of us outside of a monastic community, saying yes to walking with Jesus as part of a stable yet changing church requires humble, listening prayer and loving, embodied presence with God and each other, trusting that the same God who never changes is also making all things new.

SPACIOUS STABILITY

What spacious stability is and what spacious stability is not

A commitment to stability is not synonymous with believing our church is the right or ideal place for everyone who calls themself a follower of Jesus. Instead, spacious stability is a trust that the particular church in which God has placed us is good for God's purposes. Spacious stability embraces a holy restraint from projecting our ideals onto the church where God has placed us and trusts that—even when it feels like a painful stretch—God knows and cares about our need to feel welcomed and at home. Spacious stability allows us to wait in hope for all that God purposes for us and our church community to be accomplished.

Saying yes to spacious stability leads us to a creedal expression of faith: one Lord, one faith, one baptism, one God and father of us all. In this way, we are connected with every community of faith bearing witness to the triune God.

Saying yes to spacious stability is not the same thing as ignoring teaching, character, or actions antithetical to Jesus' teaching, character, and actions. Those who are committed to the reality of God's good church are best suited and called to address the wrongs within the church. Saying yes to spacious stability does not prevent us from walking with Jesus, who provoked holy change by sitting at tables with Pharisees, along with tax collectors and prostitutes, year after year—and then, after that, by turning over tables instead.

Saying yes to spacious stability affirms that the actual place where I worship, live, and work is where God is for me. God is in the reality of my life, not the idealized version I'm prone to wander toward.

Saying yes to spacious stability helps us walk the restful way of Jesus in all our relationships—friendship, marriage, parenting, and even our work relationships flourish with a commitment to stability. We grow in our capacity to live in contemplation and community with Jesus, others, and ourselves.

CONVERSATIO

Conversatio (conversion) means to remain open to change and is the harmonious counterbalance to the commitment of stability. We can imagine how important this commitment has been in the fifteen centuries since Benedict began forming his monasteries, and—with empathy—to the changes churches have navigated within our lifetime. As we grow in our capacity to be present in the reality of our church community, we listen for the Holy Spirit's invitations into fresh expressions of our love for God and each other. We surrender to the reality that growth is a lifelong process and that when we walk with Jesus, we are, in fact, on a journey with all the uncertainties that entails.

SPACIOUS CHANGE

What spacious change is and what spacious change is not

Saying yes to spacious change is saying yes to the tension between certainty and uncertainty. It's a willingness to be wrong and to change our minds as we listen to the Holy Spirit and our community. Spacious change embraces a holy receptiveness to new learning and expressions within the church to which we believe God has led us, and trusts that—even when it feels like a painful stretch—God knows and cares about our need to feel secure within a trustworthy community who won't seek change for the sake of change alone. We trust that God is the one who has given us the good desire to belong in a congregation that can change and grow, not at the demands of others, but for the sake of others.

Saying yes to spacious change is to embrace holy curiosity —a characteristic that nurtures and tends our commitment to further growth. We desire to retain childlike faith even as we desire to mature in the faith.

Saying yes to spacious change is to embrace the virtues of God rather than trying to signal our own. Rather than treating the church as a message board for cultural change, we welcome wholistic transformation even when the process is long and leads us on the paths of suffering that often accompany change. Saying yes to spacious change, we share in the suffering of a culture that God is making new.

Saying yes to spacious change provides a healthy balance to stability in all our relationships. We are constantly changing, and so too are the people we love. We grow more whole, not more fragmented in our love, as we embrace the realities of change. As we grow more like Jesus, we become more like our true selves, always coming full circle to belovedness.

If committing to spacious stability is being present to reality, then committing to change is being present to unpredictability. Years ago, when our oldest son was asked to pray at a family meal, he closed the prayer "Thank you for being an unpredictable God." The words took me by surprise as something I'd never thought of as one God's better qualities. Now, when I am feeling the disorientation of change, I echo Andrew's prayer: Thank you for being an unpredictable God.

Author Joan Chittister makes one of my favorite observations about what it means to embrace stability and change in the church when she says that living in this tension helps us "commit to our own adulthood,"[2] and Andrew's prayer offers a kind of response of worship to the God who fathers us into a mature relationship with Christ's church. As we walk with Jesus, we learn the rhythms of stability and change, and as we practice a Rule of Life, we make space for both. Through stability and change, we worship Jesus for being the one who laid down his life for the church and who now sits next to the Father, holding all of us together.

CHAPTER 6

BAPTIZED BELOVED

Unity in Diversity

The Father speaks, the Spirit and the Son
Reveal to us the single loving heart
That beats behind the being of all things.

—MALCOLM GUITE[1]

As Jesus was named beloved at his baptism, he invites us to share with him in the blessing of the beloved children of God. A spacious Rule of Life centers us within this baptized community and, as Esther de Waal says of the Benedictine rule, deepens our "relationship with Christ, so that the more I come to know him and to love him, the more I hope that I may become like him."[2] We've explored the paradox of a Rule of Life practiced on a spacious path: When we seek a loving God, we discover that God's love has already found us. Now I want to add to that paradox: When we seek a loving God for our true identity, we discover God's loving truth has already blessed our most authentic selves.

YOU WERE ALL CALLED TO TRAVEL ON THE SAME ROAD

The apostle Paul wrote a poem echoing the invitation to embrace our belovedness in baptism with Jesus: "Long before he laid down earth's foundations, he had us in mind, had settled on us as the focus of his love, to be made whole and holy by his love" (Ephesians 1:4, *The Message*). Before the earth's foundations, God, who was, and is, and always will be in communion with Father, Son, and Holy Spirit, had "settled on us as the focus of his love."

Paul continues to describe this spacious, united path: "You were all called to travel on the same road and in the same direction, so stay together, both outwardly and inwardly. You have one Master, one faith, one baptism, one God and Father of all, who rules over all, works through all, and is present in all. Everything you are and think and do is permeated with Oneness" (Ephesians 4:1–6, *The Message*).

Then Paul turns the conversation toward how we are different from each other, saying that just because we're called to travel the same road doesn't mean we're all supposed to look and behave the same. Made in the image of the Trinity, God calls us to live as diverse beings united in the peace of Christ.

BELOVED TRINITY

The beauty of the triune story centers on God's communal life: Father, Son, and Holy Spirit. And, so, we begin with the One who is named beloved first. The One who is Three. Blessed Trinity.

How does this relate to what it means to be beloved? For starters, to be beloved means to be made in the image of the triune God. As God is one in three, we, too, are made for the depth and breadth of communal life. We are made to give and receive love from others who are not the same as us. The eternal heartbeat of God beats to the rhythm of belovedness.

The founders of our faith described the relationship of the Trinity as a "divine dance."[3] Early church theologians described the inner life of God as *perichoresis*, which right there in the middle of the word hints at our English word *choreography*. In his book *The Beautiful Community*, Irwin Ince reminds us that "fragmentation, division, disharmony, and disunity are our story, but they are not God's."[4] Ince continues, "God is the apex of unchanging beauty as Father, Son, and Holy Spirit in eternally existent, mutually glorifying, loving, honoring, and supporting diverse community—a never-ending, beautifully choreographed dance."[5]

The Trinity exists as more than an essential part of Christian doctrine (which it assuredly is) but as the living, loving ultimate reality in which we live and move and have our being. We are welcomed to the never-ending communion of Father, Son, and Spirit and find our truest selves in their midst. We move outward, extending this hand of fellowship to the world, not as individuals but as those who have been deeply and thoroughly welcomed into the friendship of God—and abundantly refreshed to share God's love indiscriminately with the world.

BELOVED CHURCH

The church is the body Christ forms to live out the pulsing reality of the triune God in the world. While we are called to worship Father, Son, and Spirit every day and in every place, a holy reorienting happens when we gather around scripture and communion. The habits of worship we practice within our local church strengthen us to serve the common good of our cities, neighborhoods, schools, workplaces, and beyond.

We collectively make up the body of Christ and we need each other for this beautiful work.

In the book of Ephesians, we read:

> God is building a home. He's using us all—irrespective of how we got here—in what he is building. He used the apostles and prophets for the foundation. Now he's using you, fitting you in brick by brick, stone by stone, with Christ Jesus as the cornerstone that holds all the parts together. We see it taking shape day after day—a holy temple built by God, all of us built into it, a temple in which God is quite at home. (Ephesians 2:19–22, *The Message*)

In some mystical and Christ-saturated way, God places the broken up and diverse pieces that our individual lives represent to form a unified community. Like bricks in a building or stones in a mosaic, our individual gifts, and identities gather the *imago Dei* into one image of God.

Sheer genius. Spacious grace.

The beauty of our diversity is not about gifts alone. The heart of God is irrevocably intertwined with all peoples and nations. In much the same way God's image is made vivid through both the male and female of the imago Dei, God's heart is only fully recognized through the colors and textures, flavors and fragrances, stories and dance steps, personalities, and priorities of all the peoples and nations.

Whenever we are able, Brian and I love to visit churches that help us step out of our familiar worship and lean into the worship expressions of the peoples, tribes, and nations of the imago Dei. As we connect to the diverse parts of the mosaic of Christ's unified body, each part we encounter expands our imagination for the imago Dei within our congregation right now and deepens our desire for the day we will all worship together at the throne of Jesus (Revelation 7:9–12).

BELOVED *IMAGO DEI*

When the Trinity declares in Genesis 1:26, "Let us make humans in our image, according to our likeness" (NRSVue), God is deciding to make us in God's triune image. We bear God's image as a mutually loving, honoring, and supporting diverse community. We glorify God in this. And we are beautiful.

Irwin Ince defines the Imago Dei as an "overflow of God's beauty in the creation of humanity." Ince says that God brought "copies of himself"[6] into being as an overflow of the perfect love God shared as Father, Son, and Holy Spirit. The truest thing about humans is that we are made in God's image, and Jesus as both God and human is uniquely qualified to identify the most authentic parts of ourselves—the beloved person God imagined as we were being formed in our mother's womb (Psalm 139:13–16). But the invitation to recognize our true selves doesn't stop with us; Jesus calls us to embrace both our own belovedness and God's image in other humans. And so the imago Dei, at its essence, is a relational rather than an individualized identity. We are all connected; to embrace our identity is to embrace God's image in all people—including ourselves—and to reject one is to reject the other.

ONE CENTER: A RULE FOR HOLDING TOGETHER THE UNITY IN DIVERSITY OF GOD'S BELOVED COMMUNITY

In what ways do a theology of the Trinity, baptism, and the imago Dei relate to our practice of a Rule of Life?

Living in the presence of the Trinity

For a Rule of Life to be a spiritual practice it must connect us with something larger than ourselves, and since it is a Christian practice, we find that connection centered in the beloved community of God. For centuries, the circular shape of a labyrinth—one large circle making up many smaller circuits that lead to one inner center—has spoken to people of all different faiths, because most faith traditions imagine life as a spiritual journey that leads to union with a transcendent being, or god. I prefer to think that the reason for the affinity is because the image and nature of the triune God is stamped on all of us—one God, three persons calling us into a loving communion of one body with many parts. It seems we're always trying to find the most helpful symbol or metaphor to describe the Trinity.

My whole life, I've been taught the image of God as three-in-one, one-in-three. As a child, I learned the doctrine of the Trinity in terms of a metaphor: one egg with three parts: white, shell, and yolk; water as ice, liquid, and steam; an apple as skin, flesh, and seed. I'm grateful for that teaching, but it wasn't until midway into my thirties, when I was leading a worship ministry in a large church, that I began to ask questions. Questions like, "So what?" and "What difference does it make?"

As it turns out, a robust theology of the Trinity makes a world of difference in the way we worship on Sundays and in the way we live our everyday lives. In the three-personed God, we are invited, commended even, into a mystery. In this beautiful mystery is a beautiful community. The psalmist tells us that God puts the lonely into families. God, who lives and moves and has transcendent being as one-in-community, should know, God lives in the family of Father, Son, and Holy Spirit. This matters more than we imagine. If God, the Creator, identifies as a triune community, how can we—the created ones—identify ourselves as sole individuals?

All those years ago, when our family first moved to Austin, our kids began attending their new schools within a few weeks of our arrival. They didn't know anyone, and not only that, but they had left a school of hundreds to attend a school of thousands. I'm still amazed by their courage and still grieving what that courage cost them. All I knew to do to help them on some mornings as they packed their books and ate their breakfast cereal was to just keep saying to them, "You are not alone."

I told them this because I wanted to remind them that every day they are walking with an invisible company, a fellowship. I also told them this because I wanted them to be prepared to hit the intense emotion of the day, the moments they needed to decide to hide or to connect. I wanted them to imagine the presence of this community standing with them in that very moment. I wanted this talk of community to settle down deeply into their imaginations, into their souls in the very tangible, daily moments. I wanted them to grab onto the communion of the saints like a zipline plunging into the moment and swinging back up the other side, wind-blown and flip-flopped, maybe, but full of fresh energy, joy, humor, and strength.

In our first month, I wrote them a prayer and offered it as a blessing which I'm not sure they heard me say as they were stepping out the door into the unknown each morning, but maybe I was the one who needed to hear it even more:

Go with Jesus; he is with you. Also, the Father and the Spirit.
And all the people praying for you from our new church
and our old church,
and all our family and friends.

Even the angels and the saints in heaven are with you.
You are not alone.

The beauty of this spiritual reality shapes everything we are and everything we do. We are beautifully distinct as persons, yet mysteriously, and gloriously, our designed particularity never finds its identity apart from the created Whole. This paradox transforms everything. We submit every part of our lives—individually and corporately—to the three-in-one God: how we gather, how we pray, how we sing, how we make, how we intercede, how we eat, how we work and play together and alone. Knowing we are one part of a whole, created in the image of a triune God, shapes how we hear music, read books, return emails, browse social media, shop at the market, and weed our gardens. We carry with us an awareness of the entire community of God. All that we are and all that we do bears witness to the communal nature of our three-personed God who gathers us from our independent, self-referential postures into an interdependent, beloved community.

Surprisingly, many Christians not only forget the truth of our interconnectedness outside the church but carry the false narrative of a personalized relationship with Jesus into the church as well. In this false narrative, a sanctuary is just a bigger room for a privatized worship experience. Instead, in worship liturgies that remind us that we carry the image of the triune God, forming us week in and week out—one prayer, one sermon, one morsel of bread, and one sip of wine after another—we are welcomed into the full dimensions of God's beloved community. When we leave the sanctuary, we embody this loving communion, making God visible to each other and the world.

Unity of diversity in the eucharist

No act of worship combines loving, embodied presence and humble, prayerful listening more completely than the liturgy of eucharist. Week in and week out, we reenact the drama of the broken body of Christ made whole when every child, woman, and man walks to the front to receive the gifts of God for the people of God, while healing pray-ers stand by waiting for the ones who can't make it that far. I will also never forget the times I have watched our pastors serve to the end of the communion line and then, while we remained in the sanctuary savoring the wine on our lips, walked the bread and cup out to the parking lot where they knew they would find folks who just couldn't get through the barrier of the church door. This is the beauty of Jesus' body broken for us and his blood spilled for us.

The eucharistic liturgy is old and broad enough to articulate all I strove for in years of restless worship and anxious altar calls that stressed personal relationship with Jesus as something distinct from participating in God's loving communion. I have found rest knowing that no matter how convicting the sermon or provoking the altar call, at the beginning of the service, it's God the Father who gathers us; during the service, it's God's Spirit that inhabits our praises, and at the end of the service it is Jesus himself hosting the feast.

Unity of diversity in the communion of saints

I began seeking the wisdom of Christians outside of our own time and place when I began to experience the severe limitations of not understanding our place within this enormous lineage of Christianity. While the people of God in the Old and New Testament remain the foundation for understanding what it means to live in this world as a community of Christians, a whole lot has occurred between the book of Acts and now!

This desire to dig into the roots of my Christianity is what led me to appreciate things like the church calendar and classic spiritual disciplines. I'm grateful to saints and prophets from every age, and for countless contemporary teachers, poets, artists, and keepers of the faith. It's a rich heritage, and every time I hope to grow in a particular spiritual practice like a Rule of Life, I'm reminded I'm surrounded by this beloved community of the church. In my practice of a Rule of Life, I rely on the direction of people of color and other marginalized voices so that I practice contemplation and community with those who have lived different experiences than my own. I do this by nurturing real life relationships with people who are not white like me in my work, church, family, and neighborhood, by reading and studying authors and scholars from different ethnicities, and by expanding my imagination for a range of cultural expressions found in art, music, and movies. In every area of my life, a Rule of Life on the spacious path prompts me to ask the question "Who's missing from this conversation?"

Because we live with Christ in community, we cultivate a Rule of Life in ways particular to us and to our local congregation, as well as to the work of the global and historic church. We locate our stories as part of a community of loving, embodied presence with God, each other, and our full-dimensional human selves. We locate our true stories wrapped up in God's grand story. Centering a Rule of Life in the baptized community of God has helped me welcome my own story of being named Beloved.

CHAPTER 7

CENTERING IN
THE BELOVED

Things fall apart; the center cannot hold.

—W.B. YEATS[1]

It is an easy lie that has wormed its way into my mind: I am the center that must hold.

—KATE BOWLER[2]

Centered in God's belovedness, a Rule of Life makes space for us to freely examine the ways we have felt disconnected from loving communion with God and others. We spend so much of our lives trying to solve the riddle of our true selves, searching for the unique name buried underneath a center that has not held. We turn this way and that, trying to hear our name, and God has already said it. We are beloved.

BELOVED IS MY TRUE NAME

I love the name my parents gave me. *Tamara* is a Hebrew word for palm branch, which evokes something living, green, life-giving, sturdy but a little bit exotic. Palm branches are most famous in the Bible for their role in Jesus' triumphal entry, when the crowds used them to fashion a path for the man they hoped would rescue them. I think about my name every Palm Sunday when we wave our palm branches in church, and every Ash Wednesday, when the priest marks our forehead with the ashy residue of last year's palm branches. I've come to understand myself as a living *and* a dying palm—both used for the glory of Jesus, who lived and died and lives again so that I could live into my truest name, Beloved.

Early in my thirties, during a long season of healing from childhood trauma, I began to sense new freedom in my relationship with God. Reading scripture from a heart that knew belovedness rather than shame opened a whole new dimension to my relationship with God. Time in prayer began to feel like quiet, shared secrets with a trusted friend, a friend who would only love and never betray me. I filled piles of journals with words of hope, love, and desire untainted by the shame that had followed me for decades. The knowledge of belovedness moved from my mind—studiously steeped in scripture and church tradition—and moved into my heart in a bloom of loving passion for God, others, and wonder of all wonders, for my own self. I sensed in my deepest being that God was present: inviting and initiating intimacy. This is no small miracle for someone who has suffered abuse due to false and predatory intimacy. I experienced the Holy Spirit opening my heart to the joy of knowing and being known by God and others. My sense of worth expanded under the care of God's lavish love and affection. I felt light and joy in the safety of God's love. I knew—body and soul—that I was beloved.

Returning to my religious false self

Unfortunately, I began to feel like it was a bit too much. In the light of God's lavish attention, I panicked. To feel less vulnerable but still beloved, I began to treat the gift of God's attention as a kind of spiritual commodity to trade in for human attention. As I continued to spend large amounts of time reading scripture, journaling, and basking in God's presence, I found myself adopting a kind of super-spiritual-ized false self that I could trade in for validation from other people—especially spiritual leaders whom I longed to impress. Eventually, my need for human approval led me to idolize and idealize some unsafe spiritual leaders who wounded me.

This all happened almost two decades ago, and in the years since, I've often felt like I disqualified myself from intimacy with God, that the spacious path is not open to me, and that I need an alternate route. It's been hard to trust myself in the presence of God and others. On many days, the idea of inti-macy with God still frightens me. I've needed the Holy Spirit to minister more and more healing, to make space for me to accept the simple fact of my belovedness without attaching demands for human validation.

Root of religious false self is a fear of being fragile

For the first thirty years of my life, I lived with the unex-amined belief that my name was Alone and Unprotected. I sensed that instead of beloved, I was fragile, maybe not even worth protecting, because I was sexually abused when I was a little girl. I'm guessing that no matter your life story, you have reason to believe that you are fragile, too. Suffering has a way of doing this to us. We ricochet between the coping methods of anxious hypervigilance or stoic stiff upper lip to disguise our fear and shame. At its root, the belief is the same: we are alone and unprotected. Marketing campaigns, political campaigns, and—sadly—religious campaigns profit off our willingness to believe that we are alone in our vulnerability and must protect ourselves at all costs. We swallow the premise of these campaigns for an understandable reason; there are so many ways for humans to hurt each other, so much senseless tragedy, disease, poverty, and crime, and so many social critics offering to analyze the statistics of our fragmented world. It's easy to accept our role as the target audience for vulnerability-protection schemes.

When we buy into the notion that we are alone in our vulnerability—or the flip side, that we are somehow uniquely invulnerable to suffering—our ability to discern true danger from ordinary danger gets mixed up. So does our ability to discern true love from false. Out of the need to keep our sanity amid a capricious and predatory world, we create a complex system of coping skills for ourselves and the people we love. You might consider these coping methods as a burdensome system for self-protection, rather than unforced rhythms of rest and grace. If your responses look anything like mine, this "how to keep safe because I am so unprotected" default rule of life might sound familiar:

- Keep secrets, intend to take them to my grave
- Hide in shame and self-protection
- Avoid confrontation and conflict, at all costs
- Quickly resent and overreact
- Fight the wrong enemies
- Paralyze myself and my relationships with hypervigilance, or alternatively, let them wither from neglect
- Get sidetracked by inane controversies, click-bait rhetoric, and conspiracy theories
- Cloak all my true feelings, thoughts, desires, and needs in the language and disguise of a super-spiritualized, religious false self

Most damaging of all: when I believe I am alone in my vulnerability, all my energy for giving and receiving loving communion with God and others is spent on protecting myself. I am not free to respond to Jesus' invitations to come to him to rest in the unforced, life-giving rhythms of God's beloved community.

THIS IS MY BELOVED

Jesus began his public ministry on earth centered in the belovedness of God. And the thing we often forget is that, at least publicly, Jesus hadn't *done* anything yet. His first act of public ministry was stepping into baptism and hearing the Father speak his identity: "This is my Son, the Beloved, with whom I am well pleased" (Matthew 3:17 NRSVue).

Every time I read this story, I think of the old Sunday school song, "His banner over me is love." The song is based on Song of Songs 2:4, which the NRSVue translates, "He brought me to the banqueting house, and his intention toward me was love." Thinking about it now, that's probably the best Sunday school song ever. In our congregation, the children spend the first and last part of the service in the sanctuary with us adults. During the sermon, they go to Sunday school, but we always want them to know that we'll miss them while they're out of the room and that we're all one church together, so when it's time for them to leave, we sing a special song reminding them they are children of the living God who loves them very much.[3] This love that sings over beloved children is the same spirit we witness at Jesus' baptism: *This is my beloved Son, my intention toward him is love. Sing to the living God.*

In the Gospels, the second time we hear God's passionate persistence in naming the beloved is in the transfiguration account. Once again, God named Jesus, but not right away.

First, Jesus prayed, and God's presence changed his appearance "like a flash of lightning." Peter responded with a religious strategy, interrupting God's display with an idea to build three tabernacles to market the event. Next, God spoke in the cloud, "This is my Son, my chosen one." Only then, Peter acknowledged his vulnerability in the presence of God. It was the voice of God's love—not Jesus' entire appearance becoming bright as the sun or the mysterious arrival of Moses and Elijah—that sent Peter face down on the ground. It was the voice of God's love that terrified him. Jesus invited his friends into this profoundly intimate encounter with God, and Peter's response feels like a lot of the ideas my religious false identity concocts to trap down the glory of God into something more manageable, something I can shrink down to my own size. My religious false self is fascinated by God's love, titillated even, but my true self responds in awe, gratitude, and humble worship. My true self welcomes my inherent vulnerability in the presence of God and waits for Jesus' assurance that I do not need to fear. The voice of God's love terrified me for a long time and occasionally still does. I'm often tempted, like Peter, to try to find a shortcut to intimacy with God, by settling for a kind of religious proximity instead. But when I allow my full, true, vulnerable self to remain present to God's loving attention, I find rest in the center of God's beloved community. The center where Jesus holds all things together including me.

The rest that comes from being loved

Our parents name us at birth, and God gives us our forever name at the second birth of baptism. In baptism, we step into the water of death with Jesus and are raised with him, the beloved. Because belovedness begins in God, we do not name ourselves beloved; instead, we receive the name—the reality of ourselves, fully seen and loved by God—as a gift. We accept *beloved* as our name, and we accept ourselves as being loved. Our temptation is to live *as if* we are beloved without letting the truth sink down into the true state of our souls. We may believe God loves us, but we haven't allowed that love to help us discover the truth about ourselves. Any rest we feel that doesn't help us discover the truth about ourselves is a false rest. Since you are reading a book about spiritual disciplines, I'd guess the religious false self might be a temptation for you, too; the one often tries to tag along with the other. May I invite you to drop the old names, come out from under the shame that tries to hinder your intimacy with God and others, and step onto the spacious path. Child of the living God, sing to the living God.

ONE LORD: A RULE FOR HOLDING TOGETHER UNION WITH GOD AND COMMUNION WITH OTHERS

Why does intimacy with God and loving communion with others matter in practicing a Rule of Life? And how, when it feels scary or when my trust has been betrayed? How can I abandon myself to intimacy with God while maintaining healthy boundaries in my relationships with spiritual leaders and others who help me hear my name as Beloved?

Discerning safe spiritual leaders

We were made to encounter, adore, and love the one true God—Father, Son, and Holy Spirit. We're created in God's image, invited into the belovedness of Jesus as God's children, and brought into union with God through the Holy Spirit. Like the disciples face down at the transfiguration, and like my own panic in response to the voice of God's love, union with God is a powerful mystery that is likely to shake us up a bit. It's a holy relationship God reserves for our relationship with God alone. (This is why marriage is considered a holy union; God makes space for humans to participate in relationship that otherwise is for God alone.) Out of God's abundant love, we carry the overflow of the mysterious union with God into a tangible communion with each other. We were designed as porous beings; as we share the body and blood of Jesus, we are able to give and receive the blessing of being named Beloved with each other. My friend Brett Alan Dewing wrote in a poem, "Come, union, make us whole."[4] Brett's poem gives me words to pray: "Come, union" and "Come, unity." Amen.

Because we can't fully understand the holy alchemy of being centered in belovedness, union with God is a mystery. We can't rationally explain the joining of our human, finite selves with the invisible, immortal God. Because we are made in God's image, we can look for hints of this union as we draw near to the imago Dei, but we can only see in part. Paul says it's like peering through a fog or looking in a mirror instead of face to face, but when "completeness" comes, we can know fully even as we are fully known. Until completeness comes, we embody a mystery that only God can fully know. When we try to know the mystery of our true selves apart from God, looking for shortcuts to replicate the blessing and validation only God has the authority to give, we will be tempted to give that authority to others.

Inviting others to help us discern a Rule of Life as a spacious path invites others to know and be truly known. It helps me to remember that whenever I seek loving, embodied presence as part of a Rule of Life, I am meeting others at the table where the Father, Son, and Holy Spirit have made a place for us. We are keepers and cultivators of the love that Jesus shares with us—love that can be received, shared, but never taken or given apart from him. There's so much freedom in this love! I am a daughter of God and share that honor with my brother Jesus. Unbelievable! While Jesus is my brother—centered in the belovedness of the triune God—he is also my King. A Rule of Life as a spacious path makes room for me to walk, linked arm-in-arm with our good Brother, while at the same time bowing at his feet. Somewhere in the middle of this place— hidden in Christ and completely alive in His presence—I can find my truest self.

In those years of learning how to receive God's loving attention that I've described above, I tried to force the love Jesus freely gave me into a strategy to promote a false religious self, to gain the approval of spiritual leaders. I tried to stay linked arm-in-arm with Jesus while bowing at the feet of spiritual leaders who I hoped would name my true self in a way that felt more manageable than listening to a God I couldn't see, and didn't fully trust. Thankfully, some of the leaders I offered my adoration were self-differentiated enough to shepherd my devotion rather than absorb it. Lamentably, some of the leaders to whom I gave my allegiance were not self-differentiated and not safe—narcissistic, even. Instead of the vulnerability that centers us in the safety of Jesus' love, I became vulnerable to deep spiritual wounding. I imagine some of you may resonate with my experience. Some of you have been blindsided by spiritual abuse, a misuse of power that came looking for you. The wounding I received was a kind of idolatry I nurtured and sought out until it became bigger than me and turned to something else. Either way, the wounds are real and painful, and I am so sorry. May you know that you are not disqualified from intimacy with God because of the sin of those who represent God.

Gently, I want to offer a bit more of my story. While I was wounded in the church by unsafe spiritual leaders, in the mercy of God, it was also safe spiritual leaders in the church who have helped me heal from the sin others committed against me. Within a church environment that honors rather than disregards or exploits my inherent vulnerability, I've been given one of the church's most valuable gifts: a loving communion of friends centered in the belovedness of Jesus, who invites our weary, wounded selves to come to him for rest. Within this safe circle of friends, good shepherds have invited me to tell my story, name the sins others have committed against me, confess and receive forgiveness for my own, and return again and again to the center of God's beloved community as my own blessed and beloved self. In prayerful listening for the Spirit's correction and healing, and in the loving, embodied presence of safe friends I have grown in discernment that provides border lines for a structured, yet spacious Rule of Life.

Through many twists and turns, God has led us to churches that are well-tended by the women and men who pastor them. While I could tell you about many gentle and humble spiritual leaders who safely care for God's beloved, I'd like to instead offer you a summary of the characteristics I've learned to notice when I'm discerning the trustworthiness of someone who holds a position of spiritual authority. Because I know him so well, I'll share this also as what I've learned about healthy spiritual leaders from watching my priest and husband, Brian. In the time that Brian has been my priest, we've been living in the same cultural and political climate as you and your church. Brian has been shepherding a congregation through two national elections, the COVID-19 pandemic, and the breaking headlines of numerous stories of sexual and spiritual abuse—including stories within our denomination. He has often reminded us that as followers of Christ we are to unify under the ascended King Jesus and to pledge our allegiance to Jesus alone. This is the first characteristic I look for in discerning safe spiritual leaders. To whom do they ask me to pledge my allegiance?

Here are a few more parts of my rule for holding together allegiance for King Jesus with loving communion led by spiritual leaders:

- They preach their hearts out every week no matter how many people are in the room (occasionally, the sermons are even outstanding). They don't need to have the last word but can trust Jesus to host all of us at the communion table.

- They often (but not always) lead smallish churches where there aren't complex layers of separation between the pastors and the congregation.

- They address complex issues like human dignity, justice, and money only as much as Jesus did in his ministry.

- They treat their families and neighbors even better when no one is looking, and they know how to take a day or two off every week. They make space for their congregation to do the same.

- They don't take themselves more seriously than Jesus, and they know how to laugh at a good joke. They invite playfulness within congregational life.

- They know how to tend to a few close friends than they tend to the expectations their congregation may place on them for relational connection. They expect and make space for their congregations to do the same.

- They model a restful, non-anxious presence[5] inside and outside the sanctuary, trusting that Jesus is responsible to hold the church together and will keep his promise for the glory of God and for the sake of the world.

This is how I've come to embrace a loving communion pastored by healthy spiritual leaders: through the small exercises and practices that, over time, create boundaried-yet-porous space for God's love to dwell in us and through us. It's been a circuitous journey for sure. Along the way, I've grown closer to Jesus, who showed us the truest parts of God through his own suffering and death and who will not waste your experience of suffering, neglect, abandonment, abuse, illness, insecurity, mess-ups, and freak-outs to redeem God's true self in you. Be gentle. Take your time. Lean into the safe borders of contemplation and community, pointing you toward the center of God's loving, restful presence. Don't go it alone.

CENTERING A RULE OF LIFE ON THE SPACIOUS PATH

One thing I ask from the LORD, this only do I seek: that I may dwell in the house of the LORD all the days of my life, to gaze on the beauty of the LORD and to seek him in his temple.

—PSALM 27:4

Read Mark 1:9–11 or Matthew 17:1–8 slowly and, if possible, out loud a couple of times. What word or phrase catches your attention? How does your body feel as you read God's voice of love blessing Jesus? What questions come to mind? In what way do you need help to hear your name as Beloved? Could you put that need into a one-sentence prayer for help?

FOR FURTHER REFLECTION

1. How would you begin to describe your experience with stability and change in the church? What is helping you to embrace both stability and change in

your current church community? What is making
it difficult?

2. How might this sentence inform your practice of
   a Rule of Life: "Spacious stability embraces a holy
   restraint from projecting our ideals onto the church
   where God has placed us and trusts that—even when
   it feels like a painful stretch—God knows and cares
   about our need to feel welcomed and at home"?

3. Chapter 6, "Baptized Beloved" invites us to contemplate the unity of diversity in God's beloved
   community, centered in the holy Trinity, and revealed
   in the church and image of God revealed through the
   imago Dei. What resonated with you as you read this
   chapter? Where did you notice resistance? Could you
   begin to name why you might be feeling that?

4. Where in your life are you connected to a community
   who embodies well the unity of diversity of God's
   beloved community? How could you invite this
   community to come alongside you as you discern a
   Rule of Life?

5. As you read about the communion of saints, who are
   the people (from this era or the ones before us) who
   have influenced you? Who do you want to follow as
   they follow(ed) Christ?

6. In chapter 7, we considered our true name as
   Beloved. How would it feel to pray this prayer:
   "God, help me become more like Jesus and more like
   the beloved person you've always imagined"?

7. As you continue to notice the everyday pattern of
   your life with gentle curiosity rather than reflexive
   judgment, what experiences or practices from this
   section feel most inviting to your Rule of Life? Share

your response with a trusted friend. Ask them to simply pray for you.

FURTHER PRACTICES FOR CONTEMPLATION AND COMMUNITY: CENTERING PRAYER AND INNER HEALING COMMUNITIES

I've needed to be deeply healed to offer a hearty yes to Jesus' invitation to walk with his church. Here are a couple examples of practices that have become essential to centering my Rule of Life on a spacious path.

Centering prayer

Settle into a comfortable position and set your timer for fifteen minutes.

Begin by noticing your body. Take some deep breaths. As you inhale, notice how the breath feels entering your lungs and expanding through your torso. As you exhale, notice anyplace you might be releasing tension. Do this a couple of times; inhale and notice, exhale and notice. Ask God to help you understand that you are in your body and in the presence of the Trinity. That you are centered in God's love.

When you sense that your body is easing into this time of prayer, choose a simple word, phrase, or verse from scripture that expresses your desire for God. Consider words that have been meaningful from this part of the book, for example: "This is my beloved." Or "Beloved." Gently repeat the word or phrase and, similarly to how you noticed your breath inhaling and exhaling, notice how your mind responds to the word you've chosen. Where do you notice your mind relaxing? Where do you notice your mind resisting? Let this word become an invitation that calls your wandering thoughts back into stillness throughout the rest of the prayer.

Take time to become aware of your emotions. What are you feeling as you enter this time of prayer—mad, sad, scared, bored, peaceful, uncertain? Simply name the emotions in the presence of God. It is not unusual for the first minutes to be filled with many noisy thoughts. Don't worry about them or pay attention to them. Let them go. Gently return your attention to the center of God's presence and love by repeating your chosen word. When your thoughts wander let them drop to the bottom of your mind. Don't go after them. Gently repeat your word to help call you back into the presence of God and into your awareness of your body. Let the word draw your attention back to Jesus. Be with Jesus. Listen. Be still. When distractions persist let one of the following options help you return to Jesus.

If distractions persist, imagine you are walking a prayer labyrinth in a church yard just beyond a busy village square. All the noise from traffic and pedestrians walking by floats through the air and over the hedgerow surrounding the quiet prayer labyrinth. As you begin to walk the circles, you are conscious of sirens or a dog barking or children laughing, but your attention is devoted to the center of the circle, and you do not let your mind follow the sounds outside. As you circle your way to the center of the labyrinth, imagine that you are drawing nearer to Jesus. Acknowledge that the noisy distractions are competing for your attention, but continually let the invitation of your chosen prayer word call you back to the center where Jesus is waiting for you.

If distractions persist, consider turning your chosen prayer word into a prayer conversation. (E.g., "Jesus, I want to hear you call me beloved, but my mind is too anxious to listen." "Jesus, help me see your belovedness in this person who has caused me grief today." Or "Father, show me your love as I worry about my finances.")

Rest in the center of God's love. Trust the Holy Spirit to hold your heart with God's.

Gently transition from your stillness and prayer. Place your hand over your heart and take a deep breath. Release any expectation on yourself to remember every thought or feeling you experienced during this time of prayer and trust that the Holy Spirit will hold within you anything God wants you to recall later. Consider the following sentence as a closing prayer: "I am beloved with Christ in God."

Inner Healing Communities

After decades of carrying deep wounds – some of them caused by the church – it was the church that first met me in my trauma. I'm not naive to the fact that my experience might be more the exception than the rule—that many churches actively resist the idea of trauma-informed pastoral care. Still, it exists, and even flourishes in many church communities. And usually, it's happening in a way few people know. Because of its confidential nature, this kind of ministry is harder to see. It doesn't attract most churchgoers, but those who have eyes to see will be changed forever; the fruit of healing will become evident in the health of the church. The care I've received within the church has influenced my decisions to also seek medical and therapeutic care outside the church, which has been an essential component to my healing—body and soul. Because Brian and I have been given such miraculous care for ourselves and witnessed it in the lives of our friends, we have made inner healing communities part of our Rule of Life, offering it in every way possible within the context of the churches we attend.

If you don't know where to find a church that nurtures an inner healing community, here are a couple of helpful resources:

- Emotionally Healthy Discipleship Course: https://www.EmotionallyHealthy.org/find-a-course/
- Be the Bridge Community Groups: https://BeTheBridge.com/groups/
- Desert Stream Ministries: https://www.DesertStream.org/

We have also arranged our lives around the rhythms of emotional and therapeutic support groups that offer loving, embodied presence in significant seasons of suffering. While we've been surrounded by the tenderest and fiercest loving support from friends, family, and church community, there is a unique and palpable grace—a communion of sorts—that we experience when we gather in shared and safe vulnerability. As we've provided care for a family member suffering serious and chronic mental illness, one such group that has changed our lives is NAMI (National Alliance for Mental Illness).[1] Dearly loved family and friends would say the same for fellowships of people who gather to share suffering and offer hope— groups like AA (Alcoholics Anonymous), Al-Anon, and grief and bereavement support groups are all examples of loving, embodied presence to help us discern and practice a Rule of Life on the spacious path.

PART 3

Keeping a Rule of Life on the Spacious Path

A rule that makes space to offer the everyday realities of our lives as ordinary acts of worship

Prepare for Part 3 by reading Colossians 1:15–20 and Romans 12:1–2.

Centered in God's beloved community, and living in Jesus' unforced rhythms of grace, a Rule of Life makes space for us to say yes to spacious work. Jesus invites us to work from a place of rest, which is a much different offer than consumer-driven messages that treat work and rest as competitive forces in a lose-lose economy. Contemplation and community help us recognize and readily respond to the God who made us and who sent Jesus to become one of us and—even in our disruptive days—holds together all we are given to be and to do. A Rule of Life helps us integrate—rather than compartmentalize—the various spheres of our lives into one ordinary life of worship.

"Making a rule . . ." spiritual director and author Margaret Guenther writes, "must have something to do with real people trying to get through their days mindfully and fruitfully."[1] I love Guenther's emphasis on "real people" desiring to live their lives, yet wonder if "getting through" our days has ever felt more unreal?

As we navigate the everyday impacts of global disruption and suffering, we're experiencing profound disorientation in the world around us and within our souls. One attention-grabbing headline published in December 2022—"School Principals Say Culture Wars Made Last Year 'Rough as Hell'"—accompanies an article by NPR writer Cory Turner that depicts the workplace tensions between principals, teachers, and students' parents, describing the level of parent/community conflict they saw during the previous year as "either 'more' or 'much more' than anything they'd seen before the pandemic."[2] In what's become known as the Great Resignation, "quit rates" reached a twenty-year high in November 2021[3]. In December 2021 alone, 4.3 million Americans left their jobs[4], and record highs continued into early 2022. Those who have remained with their jobs have navigated the moving target of workplace protocols while simultaneously "double shifting" care for children or elderly parents. Added to vocational disorientation, we're also navigating new landscapes in our relationships at home, church, and with extended family members. In his book *Fault Lines: Fractured Families and How to Mend Them*, published in September 2020, Cornell professor Karl Pillemer offers his findings from the first large-scale national survey about family estrangement. In the study, Pillemer found that 27 percent of Americans ages eighteen and older had cut off contact with a family member, which translates to at least 67 million people nationally—likely an underestimate, Pillemer said, since some are reluctant to acknowledge the problem.[5] In an op-ed for the *New York Times*, columnist David Brooks wrote, "The percentage of Americans who say they have no close friends has quadrupled since 1990, according to the Survey Center on American Life."[6]

Real people—including many of us reading this book—are finding it harder to get through our everyday work and relationships "mindfully and fruitfully."[7] Parts of our lives feel uprooted and irreparable. How might a Rule of Life help us remain present to the ordinary, everyday reality of our lives at work and home even during seasons when our lives are full of unthinkable realities? In 2021, author and Benedictine sister Joan Chittister offered this well-timed invitation:

> When old social structures are collapsing around you and new ones are badly needed . . . When your own personal spiritual life is seeking new direction and your soul is thirsting for higher and deeper purpose and pursuit, monasticism offers an age-old path still new, still vibrant.
>
> Unlike the swings toward spiritual extremism and perfectionism that shook the Church as the centuries went by, the Rule of Benedict offers normalcy as the will of God. This is a guide, a way to heaven, that asks only what is doable.[8]

To Chittister's description of the Rule as a "way that asks only what is doable," I'd add "in the reality of our lives." Bishop Todd Hunter, a spiritual leader who has deeply influenced my understanding of the restful way of Jesus, writes "Reality . . . is always our trustworthy, supportive friend. God lives and moves and has his being in that which is real. Because God dwells in reality, our relationship with him can only happen there."[9] In Romans 12, Paul summons us to offer every routine of our daily lives in worship to the God who "dwells in reality." For centuries, Christians have been using a Rule of

Life to orient them within—rather than help them escape or ignore—the reality of their lives.

It's true that when Jesus asks us to learn from him, we are surrendering to unknown, sometimes extraordinary, acts of worship. In scripture we see Jesus fasting in the wilderness for forty days, casting out demons, resurrecting the dead, and dying by public crucifixion; we understand these responses as acts of obedience and worship to God. But Jesus also lived for thirty-three years—most of it unwritten in scripture—worshiping God with his everyday working, sleeping, and eating life. The majority of our Rule of Life will consist of these ordinary activities, too. Tending to the actual shape of our everyday lives is what makes a Rule of Life a spacious and unforced path.

We have contemplated the gift of centering a Rule of Life in the belovedness of Jesus; next we will consider how we live as fully-formed humans, made for work, rest, and relationships within real constraints of our resources and time. With the Benedictine commitment to a generative connection between work and prayer, we will consider how a Rule of Life helps us integrate the parts of our lives that we tend to force into opposing dichotomies—work and rest; spiritual and secular; body, mind, and emotions. We'll consider how to embrace the various spheres of our lives as one integrated, ordinary, beloved person in God's extraordinary kingdom. Along the way, I'll share some examples of how practices of prayerful listening and loving presence have helped me say yes to a Rule of Life that nurtures spacious work and Sabbath rest.

At the risk of sounding like a Bruce Springsteen ballad, I'd like to begin by telling you how my default rule of life for work was shaped growing up in my hometown.[10]

CHAPTER 8

WORK WITH ME

Saying Yes to Spacious Work

Generativity [is] embedded in creation. And when human beings exercise the imagination, and we act upon it with love, we create something into the world that is so expansive that typical bottom-line thinking can't explain it.

—MAKOTO FUJIMURA[1]

Making a commitment to prayer and work might not sound like a revolutionary concept. Since you are reading a book about a spiritual discipline called a "rule," I'd guess you are the kind of person who regularly prays about your work life and works at your prayer life. Still, all of us are born into powerful and pervasive cultural messages about work and rest that shape our imaginations and that need consistent reforming and renewing to live in the freedom of God's Sabbath economy. I find it helpful to revisit the stories that shaped my ideas of work and rest.

WORKING FOR RETIREMENT

I grew up in a part of the United States sometimes labeled "post-industrial." Anecdotally I can tell you it meant that almost all my peers had at least one grandparent who worked for the same shoe factory during the first half of the twentieth century. Brian and I could proudly state that all four of our grandparents worked at the factory—an industry that boomed during the world wars when soldiers needed quality footwear. The houses we gathered in on Friday nights and holidays to visit our grandparents, the parks we played in after school, and the libraries we visited on rainy days could all be traced back to the industrial boom of factory workers—many of them, like my grandfather, undereducated—who were grateful for a job that could feasibly provide for a family's home and care.

Where most of my peers could name a grandparent who worked at some point for the shoe factory, it was my parents' generation that punched the time clocks at the enormous business machine manufacturer and research facilities that filled entire city blocks in our area. By the middle of the twentieth century both companies—Endicott-Johnson Shoes and International Business Machines (IBM)—had left an indelible mark on our entire region, first in jobs and the homes they helped our grandparents finance, in parks, libraries, and world-famous carousels[2], and then in the vast and vacant factory buildings sucking up acreage and potential tax revenue in our villages. One of the inventions that contributed to the founding of IBM was the Key Recorder, introduced during the Industrial Revolution's heyday and generating incredible profitability for the business that held the patent for the first machine of its kind.[3] Tracking work time became embedded in the company culture as decades of the company's employees punched in and out at the end of each shift, counting down the time to retirement. We heard stories of engineers inventing clocks to keep on their desks calculating how many minutes and hours remaining until the final clock-out to retire to the golf course or to Florida (or both).

There was a lot of goodness we received as part of this economy—for much of my life we experienced the benefit of plentiful entry-level positions as well as top-tier, high-earning positions that funded cultural opportunities, schools, and recreational facilities, and now our kids and grandkids enjoy the parks and libraries the benefactor bosses left behind. On the downside, we grew up with an artificial sense of security, expecting that there would always be a big new business to keep our area in work, benefits, and homes, and that as long as we kept punching the clock, we'd get a long retirement to enjoy and a little bit of money to hand our kids in the end. These are the ideals that shaped our understanding of work. Not all bad, not all good, and not even close to God's vision for work.

In God's economy—the kingdom where Jesus invites us to work with him—we find that the spacious path always leads through the present reality—rather than some envisioned future ideal—of our lives. God works from a place of rest, never separating the two realms. Not only that, but God transcends our cultural constructs for work time and rest, where one helps us "earn" the other. God's restful presence is among us right now—in our kitchens and classrooms, standing desks and sit-down meetings, delivery rooms and delivery trucks—inviting us to work and rest in the company of Jesus. All of this, held together in Christ, shapes the everyday acts of ordinary worship we give back to God and changes the way we work and the way we pray.

ORA ET LABORA

For monks, work and prayer are, to use the colloquialism, all of a piece. Benedictine communities are famous for the seamless way they stitch together their daily tasks within their rich practices of prayer, known in Latin as *ora et labora*—work and prayer, prayer and work. While monastic communities may have codified prayer and work, the relationship between the two go together from the beginning when the triune God discerned the order of creation and then worked to bring the cosmos into being. Made in the image of God, we do our work as an act of worship to the God who works, who makes, who labors,[4] and who invites our work into a kingdom that has no end.[5]

We're given God's resurrection spirit, yet we still live in a fallen world where work and prayer often seem at odds with each other. We're prone to get stuck between the two, filling our days with preoccupied petitions and half-hearted labor. Energized by the power of Jesus' resurrection, all work is restored to its rightful, fruitful place. N. T. Wright describes the resurrection as the genesis of the new creation, so expansive it holds together all the work we do now with our future in God:

> What you do in the present—by painting, preaching, singing, sewing, praying, teaching, building hospitals, digging wells, campaigning for justice, writing poems, caring for the needy, loving your neighbor as yourself—will last into God's future. These activities are not simply ways of making the present life a little less beastly, a little more bearable, until we leave it behind altogether. They are part of what we may call building for God's kingdom.[6]

Ora et labora provides the rhythm for committing our work to God's kingdom economy, where our work takes place before the face of God, not just in the name of God.[7] The twofold calling of listening and love we hear in Benedict's prologue are embedded in the monastic rule of work. A Rule of Life will begin to take shape as we go about our tasks prayerfully and lovingly. For example, when we ask God to bring healing, peace, and justice in the world, the spacious path will make room for us to join the work Jesus is already doing to accomplish those things. When we ask God to provide for the hungry and the sick, the spacious path will include in our prayers the real people who grow, produce, and distribute food, and the people who research and treat diseases and govern health care.[8]

Ora et labora invites us to practice the presence of God on earth as in heaven. In God's kingdom economy, our prayer and work are never lost or wasted (1 Corinthians 15:58, *The Message*) but held together (Colossians 1:15–20) and brought to a "flourishing finish" when Christ Jesus appears (Philippians 1:3–6, *The Message*), bringing with him new invitations to work with him in the new world he brings.

SPACIOUS WORK

What spacious work is and what spacious work is not

Saying yes to spacious work will help us offer our daily work—whether paid or unpaid, ideal job or just paying the bills, underemployed or unemployed—as an act of worship to the God who created us and calls us to collaborate in creating goodness and beauty in the reality of our everyday lives.

Saying yes to spacious work is saying yes to living as creators and cultivators[9]. We can offer every sort of creative endeavor—meals, stories, crafts, spreadsheets, music, gardens, scarves, woodpiles, stand-up comedy, poems, PowerPoint presentations, rock paintings, organized closets, blog posts, and more—as our ordinary act of worship.

Saying yes to spacious work is saying yes to Sabbath rest. In God's economy the two walk together hand in hand. For the same reason, saying yes to spacious work is saying yes to regular practices of soul care. As we welcome God's Sabbath rest, we will extend the invitation of rest and soul care to everyone within our spheres of influence.

Saying yes to spacious work will help us feel more keenly the injustices of forced and underpaid labor and will help us notice the dignity of the essential workers in our society. We will prayerfully work for laws and economies that allow everyone to work as the beloved imago Dei.

Saying yes to spacious work will change how we feel about scarcity and loosen our grip on recognition, achievement, and profit. We will humbly, prayerfully discern our culture's messages about work as a pathway to self-determination, and instead, in the restful way of Jesus, offer our work as an ordinary act of worship.

Recently I read a reflection on Sabbath rest that referenced Jesus' invitation in Matthew 11:28–30. The author shared commentary I hadn't heard before and can't stop thinking about now:

> In place of the word "rest," William Tyndale's early translation of the Bible has Jesus saying, "I will ease you." The idea is that we are relieved. Relieved from the duty we have felt to remain in charge and alleviate the pain and disorientation caused by the stressors of life. To be at ease includes being rescued from trouble, bother, and difficulty—the nervous, uptight way we do life. Those at ease still do good work—a lot of it. But they move at a new, graceful pace.[10]

God creates us with a great capacity for work and does sometimes ask us to do very hard and often what might feel like unrewarding tasks. But even and especially then, we come to Jesus to work from a place of rest. The visual of a yoke in other translations of Matthew 11:28–30 is helpful here: The farm implement, a double yoke, pairs a team of oxen to do heavy-duty work. Traditionally, a farmer would put a mature, well-trained ox on one side of the yoke and on the other side of the yoke the new "rookie" ox, who needed to learn and be trained and developed. In that way, when we listen for God and listen for the invitations that are being given to us, we're acknowledging that God is already at work in some way in and through our lives. And we respond by stepping into the yoke with Jesus where that work is already happening rather than pulling on our own, in our own strength or for our own agenda. Centered in God's beloved community, we never walk—or work—alone.

CHAPTER 9

SABBATH WORK AND REST

[In the image of God], our bodies move to a rhythm of work and rest that follows the rhythm originally strummed by God on the waters of creation. As God worked, so shall we; as God rested, so shall we. Working and resting we who are human are in the image of God. At the same time, remembering the holiness of the day also reminds us that we are not God: this is a commandment, not a polite invitation. Though we are made to do good work and to enjoy consecrated rest, we can be the makers of neither commandments nor days. These we receive.

— DOROTHY C. BASS[1]

Keeping the Sabbath is an essential practice for keeping a Rule of Life on the spacious path. We have arrived at yet another paradox which Jesus turns into an unforced rhythm of grace: When we seek the working and resting God, we discover that God's work and rest have already found us. Jesus, the Lord of the Sabbath, fulfilled all the laws of the Sabbath (Matthew 5:17–18) so that we are free to enter—body and soul—into the rest of God today and forever. Sabbath rest is a command rather than an invitation and, of the Ten Commandments, the one that includes the most explicit instructions.

Because we are formed in the image of a Sabbath God, ignoring the commandment to Sabbath rest hinders our true selves and promotes a false religious version of ourselves as people always busy doing the Lord's work, yet never surrendering to the Lord's rest.

HOLY LEISURE

During the summer of 2022, my husband and I began a three-month sabbatical. Amid all the goodness we'd experienced since moving to Connecticut almost seven years earlier, we had also faced—personally and globally—major disruptions and painful upheavals. Through it all, I held onto the knowledge that a sabbatical was coming and that we had a plan for rest—something tangible we could count on and prepare for in the middle of so many uncertainties. During the year leading up to sabbatical, I carried a special sense of anticipation, kind of like the feeling that Christmas is coming. Planning for our time away from work and ministry became a kind of Sabbath practice of its own as we spent chunks of Brian's days off dreaming up our itinerary—scrolling through Airbnb sites for just the right places to call our temporary homes, studying the UK railway schedules, and ordering little packing cubes so we could travel light.

Then in the last few weeks before the sabbatical was scheduled to begin, my emotions shifted; I began to feel something different from anticipation. Guilt maybe? It felt funny to talk about getting three months to do nothing when so many people we know are either exhausted from work or looking for work. Maybe what made me most uncomfortable was when people said, "You've earned this!" I cherished the heart behind their words and accepted their good wishes, but I began to worry: *Had* I earned this? I'd try to justify our sabbatical with mental calculations about the pressures of ministry work, and figured even if the other years I was a slacker, living with a pastor through a global pandemic qualified me. I squashed ideas for adding a bunch of appointments to my calendar just to make sure I'd really earned a sabbatical. Some nights, I woke up with an anxious thought: I'm not even employed by the church. I'm just a sabbatical freeloader!

I mentioned my misgivings to my spiritual director during our monthly phone call. She asked me if I could name what I was hoping for during the sabbatical. "I want to learn how to practice 'holy leisure,'" I declared. I confessed I didn't really know the actual definition for holy leisure, but I remembered[2] it had something to do with just *being*. That's all. Being. Well, not all. Being while fully, completely, totally aware that in the being I am beloved. She asked me what that might look like, and my mind imagined floating on my back in the middle of an ice-cold lake in upstate New York. She asked me to tell her more, and I thought probably the sun would be shining on my face and my ears would be partly submerged so that all the sound above the water was muffled and all the sound below the water made me feel like I was living in some kind of mythical water world. Just me and the water and the sun. She asked me where God would be. I said, "I think God's looking at me, kind of like the sun shining on my face." Then we paused for a bit, and I recognized that, in this vision of holy leisure, Jesus would be floating in the water, too. Resting alongside me. Doing nothing but being beloved.

Two weeks before the sabbatical was scheduled to begin, our daughter suffered a traumatic medical emergency. Naturally we felt overwhelmed by the fear and grief of her suffering, but we also began to wonder if God actually intended to give us the good gift of extended rest or if we had just dreamt it up ourselves. That it was, in fact, too good to be true. My previous anxiety turned to lament. On the way to church the last Sunday before we began our sabbatical, I reflected on the fact that our well-crafted plan had become more theoretical than probable. Due to the emergency, there were several hurdles to us leaving home that none of us—including our dearest family and friends—could solve. As I stood in front of the congregation to receive their farewell benediction, I shared this lament as a request for prayer. I found myself adding a statement of hope, "And yet, this seems to be God's way with us. It has always cost more than we expected and always rewarded more than we could have ever imagined. So if that's true for sabbatical, too, then something really good is about to happen."

God did clear the path for us to take the sabbatical we'd dreamed—sometimes through simple solutions and sometimes unbelievable ones. The Holy Spirit energized our family, friends, and even a few strangers to jump hurdles for us through prayer and acts of love so that we could walk freely, unhindered, on a path of deep rest. We are forever thankful and pray that, in God's beautiful economy, we'll be able to offer rest to many others with the rest we've been given (2 Corinthians 1:4).

I still feel a bit sheepish sharing our sabbatical stories, in a world where hardly anyone works in a place that regularly provides the time, money, and permission to cease their job responsibilities for an extended rest. Brian and I have taken to quickly amending all our stories with statements like "If God ever blessed us with a substantial windfall, we'd seed a foundation that granted sabbatical resources to every kind of industry." Imagine a world where not only pastors and professors, but nurses, bartenders, and postal workers get a sabbatical.

Until that happens, we practice Sabbath rest with whatever time we are given. In her work *The Spiritual Disciplines Handbook*, Adele Calhoun describes Sabbath as "God's gift of repetitive and regular rest. . . . Time for being in the midst of a life of doing . . ."[3] A pastor in our former church recently shared some statistics about our collective need to embrace being in a world that expects us to function as inexhaustible doers.[4] Studies continue to show that stress levels in our society are very high, and poor mental health in general persists[5]. Related to work, specifically:

- 63 percent of US workers are ready to quit their job to avoid work-related stress.
- 94 percent of workers report feeling stress in their jobs.
- Stagnant wages[6] and anxiety related to economic uncertainty have become the norm.[7]

Pastors themselves are no strangers to the effects of stress. In 2021, Barna Research Group reported that 38 percent of pastors had considered quitting and that only one in three were considered healthy.[8] Although many who considered quitting have stayed, the effects of stress related to the COVID-19 pandemic, worldwide political vitriol, and the general stress of pastoral responsibilities have led to burnout among many clergy.[9]

Although Sabbath rest may not be the total cure for all work-related stress, it is a spacious rule created by God for each one of us. Sabbath rest is much more than merely taking a day off; it is one of the most important spiritual practices to help us remember again and again that—apart from anything we can do or not do—our identity is found in the image of the triune God who created work and rest. In Sabbath rest, our being is recentered within God's beloved being.

SABBATH AS A HOLY PAUSE

When I think about what it means to cease doing in order to fully embrace being, I recall a profound experience of shared holy pause I experienced many years ago. One crisp October evening in upstate New York, our former church hosted a vocal recital as part of a month-long art exhibit. Approximately a hundred of us gathered in chairs around a baby grand piano we'd pushed into the large atrium of our building. The sun had gone down, and starlight flickered through the giant windows at the roofline of the cathedral ceiling. We nibbled savory finger foods in the muted candlelight and listened while our friends, former members of our city's opera company, performed an evening of song that filled the atrium with exquisite sound. As the last note of each song resolved and the pianist lifted the sustain pedal, we basked in a kind of holy hush. Even the children sat in quiet attention. The music seemed to transport us, and we needed the pause to figure out if we'd returned to the place we started from or somewhere new altogether. Maybe we should have clapped and hollered "Bravo!" but somehow silence felt like the highest compliment we could give.

Music reminds us of the power of a well-placed rest—a beat, a breath, a break—that adds beauty to everything else that comes before and after it. What if—like the holy hush at the end of each song—we offered one day a week to collectively bask in God's brilliance and beauty? What if we imagined an entire day of ceasing from work as that kind of grateful pause tuning our ears to a beauty that will nurture us through the coming six days? The worship and gratitude for the work God has just accomplished for us, in us, and through us could be our way to exclaim, "Encore! Encore!"

When the Trinity rested on the seventh day, God was doing so much more than taking a break after accomplishing some impressive work goals. God created a Sabbath world—complete, whole, at rest. Jesus fulfilled all the laws of the Sabbath as the firstborn of creation so that we could live in the Sabbath kingdom of God. A kingdom so real, it breathes life into all seven days of the week. A kingdom so generative that it gave birth to an eighth day, where Jesus, the firstborn of creation, is making all things new. In response to this, a Sabbath practice means that we take one whole day to cease work and savor being loved in God's beloved being, and that we then carry that belovedness with us into every day of our lives.

SEVEN CIRCUITS: A RULE FOR HOLDING TOGETHER SABBATH DAY WITH EVERY DAY OF THE WEEK

How can a Rule of Life help us hold together the invitation to just be while we also have much we must do? If keeping one day for Sabbath is hard, how possibly can we practice Sabbath rest every day? How can a Rule of Life help us do that?

Numbering Our Days

First let's remember that, like the Rule of Life and every other commitment we have considered, keeping the Sabbath is a grateful response to God's initiative. Bobby Gross reminds us that the Sabbath is God's gift, "a weekly blessing, a foretaste of the eternal rest to come,"[10] and not a system we can initiate to measure spiritual maturity. The unforced rhythms of freedom and commitment and the rhythms of giving and receiving love are the same rhythms Jesus invites us to follow in *being* restful and *doing* work. Listening for the invitation of Jesus puts doing in its proper place—a loving response to what God is already doing. More precisely, we respond with our being to God's being.

Rabbi Abraham Joshua Heschel described the Sabbath as a "sanctuary in time"[11] that calls the other six days of the week to worship. Evoking the Old Testament motif of exile and promised land, Heschel wrote, "The sabbath cannot live in exile, a lonely stranger among days of profanity ... the sabbath needs the companionship of all the other days."[12] Through his death and resurrection, Jesus holds together the Old Testament command to observe Sabbath, begun when God rested on the seventh day and fulfilled when Christ rose on the first day of the week (Mark 16:2)—the first Sabbath of the new creation. The architecture of the prayer labyrinth helps us envision this new way of keeping time that transcends our chronological understanding of the seven-day cycle—a Sabbath so revolutionary it ushered in an eighth day of creation. In the ancient design of the classical, or seven-circuit, labyrinth,[13] prayerful pilgrims walk seven outer circles—representing the seven days each week leading us to the center of Sabbath rest—before arriving at the eighth circle at the center and then turn around to begin again, walking outward from the eighth circle which has become the first.

While keeping the Sabbath is a weekly rhythm, a Rule of Life also helps us to keep Sabbath time within the twenty-four hours of each day. Like the origins of Sabbath rest, we find wisdom embedded in the traditions of God's people to order our daily lives within a Rule of Life. "The Hebrew evening/morning sequence conditions us to the rhythms of grace," writes Eugene Peterson. "We go to sleep and God begins his work."[14] Tish Harrison Warren delightfully expounds the Hebrew "evening/morning" rhythm that Peterson describes:

> In Jewish culture, days begin in the evening with the setting of the sun. ... The day begins with rest. We start [our day]

by settling down and going to sleep. This understanding of time is powerfully reorienting, even jarring, to those of us who measure our days by our own efforts and accomplishments. The Jewish day begins in seemingly accomplishing nothing at all. We begin by resting, drooling on our pillow, dropping off into helplessness.[15]

Circling the Sabbath, we walk day in and day out in Jesus' unforced rhythms of work and rest.

SEVEN RHYTHMS IN SABBATH TIME

A Rule of Life helps us keep practices of being and doing, lovingly discerned, within the following seven timeframes:

Sabbath: One whole day each week for just being, including practices of communion and worship, play, feasting, and rest.

Daily: Daily practices of being and doing, including practices of prayer, work, rest, scripture, relational and self-care, healing communities, and hospitality.

Weekly: Weekly practices of being and doing, including practices of prayer, scripture, relational and self-care, healing communities, and hospitality.

Monthly: Monthly practices of being and doing, including practices of spiritual direction, relational and self-care, healing communities, and hospitality.

Seasonally: Seasonal or quarterly practices of being and doing including practices such as fasting and feasting, silence and celebration, lament and rejoicing, confession and forgiveness, giving and receiving, and work and rest.

Annually: Yearly practices of being and doing including retreat, relational and self-care, and rest.

Sabbatical: One extended period of time for just being, including practices such as communion and worship, play, feasting, and rest.

CHAPTER 10

ORDINARY (AND EXTRAORDINARY) TIME

What you see in an eclipse is entirely different from what you know. It is especially different for those of us whose grasp of astronomy is so frail that, given a flashlight, a grapefruit, two oranges, and fifteen years, we still could not figure out which way to set the clocks for Daylight Saving Time.

—ANNIE DILLARD[1]

To every thing there is a season, and a time to every purpose under the heaven.

—ECCLESIASTES 3:1 (KJV)

A Rule of Life helps us keep the schedule of God's new creation where Christ holds all things together and returns it to us as a gift. "It was very good," God pronounced in Genesis, and in the mercy of resurrection, time is good again. This too is a countercultural message when time on earth is seen as something to be hoarded, snatched, preserved, or spent. "Time is the only truly scarce commodity,"[2] says the narrator on one my least favorite television advertisements, yet I wonder how many of us believe the same philosophy and how that belief might shape a Rule of Life? If we arrange our lives around the anxiety-inducing belief that time is a "scarce commodity" of which we'll never have enough, how possibly could we practice a Rule of Life on the spacious path? A Rule of Life helps us examine our beliefs in contrast to cultural messages about time that bombard us from every direction.

The good news is that God, the creator and keeper of "seedtime and harvest, cold and heat, summer and winter, day and night" (Genesis 8:21–22) transcends time. Through Jesus, who brought eternity into the exact constraints of our twenty-four hour days, God holds time together in a way that is "so spacious" and "so expansive" Paul exclaims in Colossians 1, "that everything of God finds its proper place in him without crowding" (Colossians 1:18–20, *The Message*). That belief might not prompt people to snatch up river cruises before their time runs out, but it will assuredly and blessedly invite us to practice a Rule of Life in the restful way of Jesus.

THERE IS A SEASON

In 1959, Pete Seeger, inspired by the Old Testament passage, wrote "Turn, Turn, Turn" into a song that, as of 2021, has been covered by nearly one hundred artists.[3] From the era of the wisdom writer in Ecclesiastes to the folk singers and performers in our day, humans have tried to give voice to our longing for "a time to every purpose under heaven." Seasonal rhythms like those we are reminded of in that hit song serve God's Sabbath economy, inviting us to keep company with Jesus in unforced rhythms of time. Whether it is our season of life or the season of the calendar, our days are shaped as much by what is happening around us as by what's happening within us. The temperature outside, the time of day, the new pet that needs attention, and the fasting and feasting of the

liturgical calendar all matter in our calling to live a life of contemplation and community.

Seasons of the earth

Keeping a Rule of Life that reflects the reality of the natural world around us not only invites us to rest but to live
generatively in God's good and beautiful world. The seasons
of nature, created by God, deserve our prayerful attention and
loving, embodied presence. We've already talked about how
much I depend on the seasons to orient my sense of direction
and well-being. Seasonal rhythms and practices delight me—
from the buzzy summer nights sitting around a campfire to the
snap and crackle of a hearth fire, tucked away from a snow
globe outside the front window, and everything in between.
I love reading the Old Farmer's Almanac to learn Algonquin
names for all twelve of the year's full moons[4] (my favorite is
September's Full Corn Moon).[5]

Seasons of nature fit into the Rule of Life as a spacious path
that holds together the parts of our lives most related to cultural traditions and civic holidays. For example, in the United
States, summer and autumn's civic calendars are packed with
holidays and remembrances like Memorial Day, Labor Day,
and Thanksgiving—each one inviting their own rituals and
traditions. A Rule of Life invites us to pay attention to the
neighborhood block parties, town fairs, barbecues, and family
vacations, and to soak up all the common grace of the place
and time in which we live.

Seasonal rhythms also invite us to live on the human scale
God intended. My friend Amy and I joke that we may be the
only two people in the United States who celebrate the end
of daylight saving time each autumn. We love the permission
it gives us to tuck into winter's invitation for longer hours of

rest and sleep, and scientific data seems to be on our side. In 2020, the American Academy of Sleep Medicine called for a ban to end daylight saving time for good,[6] citing findings from twenty-five years of studies that support keeping standard time year-round because it "aligns best with human circadian biology and provides distinct benefits for public health and safety."[7]

In *Wintering: The Power of Rest and Retreat in Difficult Times*, Katherine May writes like she's been eavesdropping on my conversations with my friend about daylight saving time: "[In November] as soon as the sun goes down, I start thinking about bed . . . My instinct is to hibernate the evenings away."[8] Her book, written pre-pandemic but released in the first fall of our globally enforced hibernation, struck a chord with readers facing a winter like none they'd ever experienced. Her stories draw from her love for shorter winter days, but also from the lessons she's learned in seasons of suffering, including years of major depression which eventually led to an Asperger's diagnosis. In May's understanding, winter is a season to embrace rest and seek restoration for the cold and harsh realities of our world. "Plants and animals don't fight the winter," she writes, "they don't pretend it's not happening and attempt to carry on living the same lives that they lived in the summer." [9]

Wintering is, of course, a book about more than one of nature's seasons. It's an invitation to live into the reality in which we find ourselves. And to do this, May says, "we need to address our very notion of time. We tend to imagine that our lives are linear, but they are in fact cyclical . . . we pass through phases of good health and ill, of optimism and deep doubt, of freedom and constraint."[10] In other words, May is reminding us that "for everything there is a season."

Seasons of Life

Seasons of life is a phrase we use to describe the cycles of stability and change that, perhaps more than any other dimension of time, give shape to our Rule of Life. In his book *Let Your Life Speak*, spiritual writer and teacher Parker Palmer describes the value of language to illustrate the rhythms of our lives.

> Seasons is a wise metaphor for the movement of life, I think. It suggests that life is neither a battlefield nor a game of chance but something infinitely richer, more promising, more real. The notion that our lives are like the eternal cycle of the seasons does not deny the struggle or the joy, the loss or the gain, the darkness or the light, but encourages us to embrace it all—and to find in all of it opportunities for growth.[11]

My understanding of seasons of life is profoundly influenced by my calling as a mother. In 1997, I had just given birth to my fourth child in six years, a calling better than I'd ever dreamed and harder than I'd ever imagined. I didn't even realize the rarity of this gift I'd been given, but I was grateful. And really, really tired. I've kept countless photos from the years my children were young, in dozens of scrapbooks that line my bookshelves. I revisit them on each of my children's birthdays, on milestone days like graduations and weddings, and on days my children are suffering beyond the reach of my care. The photos remind me of a stage of life that stretched me—body and soul—almost beyond recognition.

One photo that has earned a kind of iconic status features my two-year-old daughter and four-year-old son standing on the front stoop of our rental house. My little girl's face is smeared with hot-red lipstick, and my little boy is scowling at the camera, both sporting autumn jackets haphazardly slung over their saggy pajamas. They are clearly posing as hostile witnesses to a morning when everything that could have gone wrong did, beginning with that lipstick and ending with a dash to get my oldest son to school after he missed the bus. With our youngest baby girl on my hip, I tossed the two grumpy preschoolers into our minivan, unable to respond to their protests against their hurried lot in this world. What I wanted to say was "Me too, darling. Me too." What I probably said was "Hurry, hurry! We're late!"

Once we had safely delivered my oldest son to school and returned home, I made the preschoolers wait on the porch while I grabbed the camera off the hook in the coat closet, knowing that someday future me would be grateful for the memory, even if the present me might have felt like falling into a sobbing lump on my bed. Mercifully, I didn't photograph all the times I'd scolded my kids when they dumped breakfast cereal on the floor or the times I'd ungently plopped them in their beds for naps because, more than anyone else, I needed some peace and quiet. I certainly would not have taken photographs of us all lined up in our church row, my husband and me with our four children ages six and under, me too proud to take our wriggling toddlers to childcare because I wanted so badly to look like the other rows of well-groomed families in our congregation who sat together for the entire service. (I swear I saw their four-year-olds taking sermon notes!) I don't have photographs of those moments, but I recall them in bouts of regret and healing confession. I'm wise enough now to know the rarity of this gift—the forgiveness I've received from God and my children. It is a treasure more precious than all my photographs combined, yet one I hold close to my heart much the same way.

When I look back through the notes I penned in our family scrapbooks—in between the lines of the super-spiritualized language of my false religious self—the voice of my true self breaks through here and there in penned snatches of scripture, poems, and stories I wanted to remember for our family. One prayer, adapted from some life-changing books I'd read by Brennan Manning, shines off the scrapbook pages as a benediction on that season of my life and serves as a reminder for the one I'm living now:

> Father, please let the Murphy family live lives soaked in prayer and centered in Jesus. Let us always keep in mind that we are flawed and allow us to laugh often and easily at ourselves and any creeping pretensions of "holiness." Please help us to trust always in letting ourselves be loved by God as more important than loving God in some kind of mechanical way. Please help our family to never distort the face of a beautiful God.[12]

I didn't know about the spiritual practice of a Rule of Life until my children were grown, but in hindsight I can see the times the Spirit gave us the kind of wisdom and grace a Rule provides.

It is in the nature of seasons to change. At times this can feel reinvigorating—like a clean notebook at the beginning of a school year. At other times, change can feel overwhelming, even grievous, as we cling to the old while fearing the new. Compounded by the change of my husband's new job across the country and our children leaving home at the same time, entering the season known as "empty nest" felt like a kind of suffering as hard as anything I'd ever felt in those early years of motherhood. To find some stability during so much loss and change, I unconsciously reverted to old patterns, placing unrealistic expectations on myself to finally accomplish all the things I always said I could do if only I had the time to myself instead of parceled out among my children.

What a disappointment to discover that even in a house where I could organize my belongings exactly the way I liked without four other humans disturbing them, and even with a schedule that felt like a clean slate compared to the one I used to keep for six people, I felt overwhelmed and interrupted every day. In the relative peace and quiet of this new season of life, my inner world was noisier and more distracted than ever. The rhythms of my days devolved into a weird mix of busywork and inertia; I woke up each morning with the knowledge that I could pray without interruption and found myself falling into internet conspiracy theories instead. It turns out that the biggest challenge to my sense of meaningful accomplishment is me. I am a late bloomer when it comes to the kind of self-awareness people who live alone already know in all the best and hardest ways. While I would have preferred to discover the rich reward of practicing a Rule of Life when I was much younger, it arrived—like my encounter with the prayer labyrinth in Texas—at the time I was most desperate and most open to welcome it. And like the prayer labyrinth, I discovered—after some trial and error—that a Rule of Life can act as a spacious pathway that unwinds the disorientation that accompanies the changing seasons. Keeping a Rule of Life has helped me keep moving in the direction of Jesus, others, and myself through all kinds of societal and personal disruption—financial strain, multiple moves, caring for family members suffering acute illness, starting new jobs, navigating painful political controversies that threatened our church community, hosting my children's weddings, and becoming a grandparent, to name a few things. A Rule of Life helps me map the practices of listening and love that route and reroute me through the ubiquitous detours of my days. It helps me orient my life in the restful way of Jesus.

You are in a season of life right now. It might be parenting young children like me all those years ago or an empty nest like me now. You might be in a season of life shaped by the ailments of an aging mind and body that slows your pace and disorients your relationship or in a season of just starting out—fresh-faced and frightened by your new job, new hometown, or new church family. Maybe death or divorce or a medical diagnosis have forced your life to a hard stop, or maybe you're living in the long limbo of hope deferred—the infertility treatments that don't take, the creative project that keeps getting delayed, or the funding for an education that keeps falling through. Most of you are probably living somewhere in between, yet even then, you know change is going to come. What if we could embrace the reality of change rather than try to flatten its impact in our everyday lives? A robust Rule of Life—empowered by the Holy Spirit and kept in the company of Jesus and others—makes space for us to change and grow. In a world constantly in flux, when what we do with our days changes so dramatically that we forget how to be, a Rule of Life returns us to the center of God's beloved being where we find our own.

Liturgical seasons

Like the practice of cultivating a Rule of Life, the liturgical year— beginning with Advent and moving all the way through each week of Ordinary Time—is another structure that has invited me into unforced rhythms of Sabbath time. Keeping the church calendar invites me to order my Rule of Life within a common rule for the historical and global church—a practice that shapes God's beloved community together into the grand narrative of God's never-ending kingdom. Theologian and author W. David O. Taylor describes keeping the rhythms of the church calendar as living in "subversive time"[13]—time that simultaneously counters the narrative of a consumer culture and aligns us with "something bigger than ourselves."[14] The church calendar—beginning with Advent in late autumn rather than January 1 of the civic calendar—is "a subversion of time as we know it."[15]

Taylor continues:

> For Christians, as the German theologian Karl Barth reminds us, time occurs in the "sphere of grace," not in an economy of scarcity. At the Fall, humanity becomes lost and tumbles into lost time. Fallen into sin and isolated from God, humanity now experiences time as distorted and frustrating. But even as time begins in grace, so God in his covenant offers again to humanity the "time of grace."[16]

N. T. Wright describes the invitation to return to a "time of grace" with the metaphor of setting a watch to a new time zone.[17] As the first disciples "set their watches" to the Sabbath time of the new creation—initiated when Jesus was resurrected on the first day—everything about how they measured time changed. Wright notes, "Within two or three generations, this sense of living in a new time zone developed its own new styles of annual celebration."[18] This "annual cycle," as Wright describes the liturgical calendar, "became a way of telling the all-important story" of God's kingdom arriving on earth as it is in heaven. Embedding the practices of the liturgical year within a Rule of Life helps us set our watches to the new time zone of God's "final new creation."[19]

FOLLOWING THE RHYTHMS OF JESUS' ORDINARY AND EXTRAORDINARY LIFE

Keeping a Rule of Life in the rhythms of the liturgical year makes space to practice "every purpose under the heaven" (Ecclesiastes 3:1, KJV) and teaches us in real time all the vital practices of Christian discipleship and worship expression. In its simplest form, "liturgy" means "the work of the people." To practice the liturgical year means that together, we offer God the full range of worship expression that Jesus and his church have taught us—rhythms of celebration and lament, silence and joyful noise, fasting and feasting, confession and forgiveness and more.

It was my learning about the church liturgical calendar and the classic spiritual disciplines that most helped me understand my need for a Rule of Life. As I've mentioned, my bad habit of operating out of an "all or nothing" mentality led me to believe that I needed to learn all the disciplines simultaneously, and short of that goal, to attempt none of them at all. I wanted to learn how to fast, keep silence, feast, lament, make confession, give alms, pray the church prayers, and celebrate the lives of the saints all at the same time. Keeping the liturgical year invited me into unforced rhythms of learning and practice. Each year at Lent, I learn a little bit more about what it means to fast, make confession, and give alms; in Eastertide, I shout my alleluias a little bit louder and add one more dessert to the feast. I've discovered that the rhythms of the earth and church guide me toward a healthy moderation in all things, so that, season after season, year after year the broad scope of spiritual practice begins to feel more familiar. My emotional and physical muscle memory moves me forward with the church calendar in more organic and less self-conscious movements from one worship discipline to another.

Music director and mother Amanda McGill describes her experience coming to the liturgical year after being formed in a church background that did not recognize the church calendar. She writes, "the historical church year was a compelling, but foreign concept. Our priest . . . often says that it takes around ten years for the church year to get in your bones, deeper in your yearly rhythm than the secular calendar."[20] From my family's experience, I'd agree with Amanda's priest—a decade for the church year to "get in your bones" sounds about right. We've been rehearsing the prayers and practices of the liturgical seasons for a little more than a dozen years now. A few years in, I noticed that we'd begun to feel a little bit less self-conscious as we lit the candles and wore the ashes, and around the decade mark I noticed we'd begun to carry the palms and the alms with a comfortable grasp rather than gingerly handling them as a rarity, something too *other* or precious. We've learned that it's the repetition of the liturgical calendar—not the discarding of it—that teaches us not to take it too seriously.

SEVEN SEASONS: A RULE FOR HOLDING TOGETHER ORDINARY AND EXTRAORDINARY TIME OF THE CHURCH CALENDAR

How can following the historic church calendar inform a Rule of Life on the spacious path?

Keeping liturgical time

The liturgical calendar that the church has developed over centuries—which also happens to be shaped like a prayer labyrinth[21]—works in partnership with a Rule of Life. I may not remember exactly each item on my list, but I know that if it's Lent, my days are arranged around the church's rule of simplicity, confession, and fasting. If it's Christmastide, our calendar is filled with feasting, celebration, and play.

Even if your church follows the civic calendar more prominently than the liturgical, you can join in with your brothers and sisters in Christ across the globe from the quiet spaces of your own home. You could create—figuratively or even literally—a family altar. This does not have to be elaborate, time-consuming, or expensive. Simple tangible acts will impress themselves upon your hearts and minds for a lifetime: a book or two filled with rich images and time-tested writings, mealtime prayers, a candle or two. If this all sounds impractically holy, I assure you the best sort of liturgical worship happens when we carry humble, prayerful listening and loving, embodied presence through the ordinary and extraordinary time of the church calendar. Year after year, we live into the truest versions of ourselves within God's beloved community.

SEVEN SEASONS OF THE LITURGICAL YEAR

Advent begins the church calendar and invites us to watch and wait for the three arrivals of Jesus—first as the long-awaited Messiah, as God-with-us now, and last as the returning, triumphant King. Simple preparation and reverent anticipation characterize the prayers and practices of Advent, which include invitations to silence, simplicity, intercession, confession, and almsgiving.

Christmastide follows the quiet prayer of Advent with an outburst of joyful noise and festal abundance. For twelve days, beginning with the Feast of the Incarnation on December 25 in the Western church, we celebrate the miraculous arrival of the Messiah. Savory feasting and childlike delight characterize the prayers and practices of Christmastide, which include invitations to celebration, thanksgiving, play, peacemaking, and generosity.

Epiphanytide follows Jesus' ministry on earth, beginning with the story of his baptism and culminating with the story of his transfiguration. The third season of the church calendar begins with the Feast of Epiphany on January 6, to celebrate with the Magi the arrival of Jesus as the revelation of God to all nations. Joyful witness and renewed commitment characterize the prayers and practices of Epiphanytide, which include renewing our baptismal vows, bearing witness to Christ's light and life in the world, blessing our homes and neighborhoods, and acts of healing and justice.

Lent begins with Ash Wednesday and continues for forty days (excluding Sundays) through the end of Holy Week. Sober reflection and acts of repentance characterize the prayers and practices of Lent, which include invitations to fasting, confession, almsgiving, and lament for the suffering of our neighbors, ourselves, and the whole world.

Eastertide, beginning with the Feast of the Resurrection and including the Feast of the Ascension, lasts for fifty days. Exclamatory worship and celebratory feasting characterize the prayers and practices of Eastertide, which include invitations for baptism, thanksgiving, savoring beauty, feasting, play, and caring for creation.

Pentecost begins fifty days after Easter and marks the day the Holy Spirit was given to the church. Thanksgiving for the gifts of the triune God and passionate, outward-facing practices and prayers characterize the prayers and practices of Pentecost, which include invitations to renew our commitment and gratitude for God's baptized, beloved community, repentance of the divisions within the church, reconciliation, discernment of our gifts and callings, and acts of expansive mission in the world.

Ordinary Time is the longest season of the church year, filling the months between Pentecost in late spring and Christ the King Sunday on the final Sunday before Advent. Sabbath rest, generative work, and loving embodied presence with Jesus, others, and ourselves characterize the prayers and practices of Ordinary Time.

CHAPTER 11

ORDINARY DAYS

If I am to spend my whole life being transformed by the good news of Jesus, I must learn how grand, sweeping truths—doctrine, theology, ecclesiology, Christology—rub against the texture of an average day. How I spend this ordinary day in Christ is how I will spend my Christian life.

—TISH HARRISON WARREN[1]

Don't let me miss the road signs you've posted. . . . Train me in your ways of wise living.

—PSALM 119:9–16 (*THE MESSAGE*)

A Rule of Life makes space for us to integrate the spheres of our everyday work and relationships into one ordinary life of worship. As we pace our Rule of Life to the seasons of the church calendar, we might wonder what to do with expanse of days set apart by the church as Ordinary Time. A helpful place to begin answering this question is by prayerfully considering the parts of Christ's life that scriptures tell us almost nothing about. You could say that the years between his toddler days, which were spent migrating to various parts of the world as his parents sought refuge from Herod, to the beginning of his more formal ministry, marked by his baptism in the Jordan

River, were the Ordinary Time of Jesus' life, as they make up the majority of all of his days on earth.

What does it mean that half of our calendar is left open to the ordinary? What does it tell us about the God who created and gives purpose to our lives? If the historic liturgical calendar teaches us to number our days to gain a heart of wisdom, there must be a lot of wisdom to be gained in our regular working, resting, and worshiping lives. In this chapter, we'll consider the familiar pathways of our ordinary lives as the exact place Jesus is inviting us to join him in work and rest, and the place we joyfully offer the quotidian bits and pieces of our days to God as an act of worship (Romans 12:1).

ROUTES AND ROUTINES

I learned a long time ago that as soon as I figured out a routine for one part of my life, another thing would quit working altogether. I began to put the word *routine* in the same category as *tips*, *techniques*, and *Spanx*—all have their place, but they also have a limited lifespan. But the word *route* I can get behind. A familiar pathway, a preferred direction from one point to another—I can work with that.

With every move we have had to make in the thirty-plus years of our marriage, I've spent almost as much time scoping out the walkways around each potential house as I have the number of rooms and bathrooms and kitchen cupboards in the house itself. It's not just that I want to know what resources will be available to us in any given neighborhood, but subconsciously I'm trying to discern what *story* we're potentially moving into. We've been blessed to move into a full range of storied living arrangements—from the quiet suburban backyards where our kids spent hours each day jumping on a trampoline with their friends, to the places we moved within walking distance of school to save on car and fuel expenses, to the loft apartment in a nineteenth-century corset factory whose front door led to a large parking lot where we regularly congregated with dozens of neighbors in the middle of the night because of a glitchy fire alarm system. Nature essayist Scott Sanders gives me words to describe my compulsion to forage for meaning outside the front door of each home we've considered:

> The likeliest path to the ultimate ground leads through my local ground. I mean the land itself, with its creeks and rivers, its weather, seasons, stone outcroppings, and all the plants and animals that share it. I cannot have a spiritual center without having a geographical one; I cannot live a grounded life without being grounded in a place.[2]

When we realized the loft apartment in the corset factory wasn't quite the right fit for our family (pun intended), God provided us with a rental house in a neighborhood whose "local ground" surpasses everything I've ever dreamed about: friendly, unpretentious houses and multifamily dwellings, vibrant coffee shops and quirky bars, three parks within walking distance, two of which curve around the rocky shoreline of the Long Island Sound. Our friends, who moved from the lonely neighborhoods of pandemic-era Manhattan, in part so they could be our neighbors, use the words of the psalmist to describe this area known as Black Rock: "The boundary lines have fallen for [us] in pleasant places . . ." (Psalm 16:6, NRSVue).

Year-round we walk the boundary lines of this "pleasant place," reconnecting the spiritual ground of our lives with the geographical ground of our neighborhood. No matter the season, when I walk our neighborhood, I become a recipient of so much goodness. Almost immediately, I greet the fresh air in my lungs and reinvigorated blood pumping through my body like sleepy co-workers who just got caught napping on the job. Every part of me snaps to attention, noticing new color, smells, and sounds like someone has just autocorrected the brightness level of my sensory filters. On particularly good walks, I notice a stirring gratitude and desire to pray for others and the earth itself. I pause at the little free libraries that dot our neighborhood, smile at the dogs wearing ridiculous sweaters, admire the anonymous art installations that pop up in chalk drawings and stone cairns along the shoreline, and chat with elderly neighbors sitting alone on park benches. On summer Saturday mornings, Brian and I walk a few blocks to the farmers market, sometimes pushing our grandson in his stroller, which we then fill up with armfuls of corn on the cob that tickle Julian's face with their silky stalks. We get to know local creators and cultivators and learn to appreciate their skill in growing the ingredients we'll add to our salads and roast on the grill. As September arrives, we buy less fresh produce and more apple cider doughnuts, because living in New England demands it.

But we also meet our neighbors and hear the stories they care about on any given week. The interaction often moves us into practical action as we discover ways to become invested in our local businesses and care for the natural resources of our neighborhood; we sign up to help clean the beaches at the neighborhood park, over tip at the coffee truck, drop money in the buskers' hats, and leave with a bouquet of wildflowers that we bought to support the nearby food shelter.

The routes we walk—rhythms of embodied presence and prayerful listening to the small world outside our front door—help me to notice the small, and not-so-small, shifts in our season of life. Like the winding pathway of a prayer labyrinth, the familiarity of the route around the neighborhood invites me to engage my body while freeing my heart and mind to reflect and pray.

During a period when our family experienced prolonged and intense suffering and grief, I was holding my breath emotionally, just trying to get through the day without feeling too much anxiety or anything else. I didn't fully realize I was living this way until I was midway through one of my walks. The sights that would usually rouse a sense of hope and gratitude— happy gulls dropping clams on the rocky shore when the tide is out, the briny whiff of the sea air making my eyes water, or the chatter of neighbors resting on park benches shading their eyes from the sun reflecting off the water—felt flat. More than flat—heavy, burdensome even. In that moment, I became aware that I'd been keeping my head down, trying to just get through the walk while resisting the beauty around me, and that this had significant consequences for my spiritual life.

Beauty invites in us equal parts longing and contentment— neither pair well with trying to press the pause button on our emotions. Realizing this didn't lift the pain, but it did elicit a sense of tenderness toward myself: I realized I was deep in grief and needed mercy. For a long season after that, my walks mostly consisted of me asking God to make me able to sense the merciful mystery of Christ's presence ahead, behind, above, and below me, even though I was too sad to savor the beauty. As this awareness grew, gratitude again stirred in my weary heart. I felt grateful.

The routines of the walk change with the seasons, but the route always grounds my story in the story of this place. I don't know how long we'll be given to live in this neighborhood; we don't own the house we live in, but if the day comes for us to find another neighborhood, I'll be searching out the story lines of a new place, finding the route that will lead me home.

FAMILIES, FRIENDS, AND NEIGHBORS

As part of our worship liturgy following the sermon each Sunday, we pray for the church, world, and our community in a particular way, known as the Prayers of the People. In one part of the prayer, the person leading says, "In peace, we pray to you, Lord God. For all people in their daily life and work," and together as a congregation, we respond, "For our families, friends, and neighbors, and for those who are alone."[3] There are a few variations for this liturgy, but this version is my favorite. I love the cadence and comprehensiveness of this little litany that holds together the relationships that make up our daily lives and provide the "local ground" of our life story.

The relationships of family, friends, and neighbors populate almost every part of a spacious Rule of Life. I could write an entire book for just this section because these relationships—the people with whom we share the most ordinary and extraordinary seasons of our lives—are inextricably intertwined with our understanding of our true selves and of the shape of our work in the world. For now, I'd like to share one learning from my own life for each of these four groups of people who have seen the best and worst versions of me and who have helped me to form a more spacious understanding of the nature of love in the reality of my daily life.

Spacious family

I know, I know—if you're a parent, old ladies have stopped you in the store to warn you that the time flies by faster than you can imagine and that you need to make the most of every single moment with your cherubs. I've discovered that that's sort of true. Most true, though, is that Jesus is a redeemer of time. It's taken a couple of decades, but I can see how God has been answering the prayer that our family's way of being reflects, most importantly, the God who loves us tenderly. I am now a grandmother who sits nearby and tries to offer a restful presence. I watch my daughter Kendra and son-in-law Jordan care for our first grandson with a kind of ease we barely understood as new parents decades ago. I watch in awe and notice God has arrived in their peaceful, patient attention to Julian. I have not missed it. God moves outside of time and space, God returns time and stretches it out in just the right ways so he can save us all.

As I become the old lady stopping young parents in the grocery store, I'm trying to say instead: Don't worry. You've got time, and it's going to take time.

In those years I described earlier where I forced routines on my family that were ill-fitting and burdensome for them (and for me), I was living in false narrative where the terms *mother* and *pretensions of holiness* were synonymous. I thought I was supposed to be straitlaced and spit-spot. I thought my role in the family was to nurture an enclosed breeding ground for spiritual perfection, which resulted in forced routines and anxious attention toward my children and husband. What I have learned—so often the hard way, and so often because of the gracious forgiveness of my husband and children—is that a family is not a place of enclosure but instead an outpost of welcome and a nurturing place to live a loving, embodied presence in the literal world around us. Spacious families are formed with the same practices that help us discern the spacious path of a Rule of Life—through ordinary practices of humble, prayerful listening and loving, embodied presence. Understanding that my nuclear family is not the center point around which God's kingdom orbits invites me to envision walking through each season of my life in much the same way I might circle a prayer labyrinth—often feeling like I'm walking in circles and never getting anywhere, yet held by a spacious path directing me in the way of Jesus and others—including, and in precious, particular ways, my husband and children.

More than ever—as the world continues to experience relational and geographic fragmentation—we need to expand our understanding of family. When Jesus called his disciples, he always called them to leave everything behind including their families. We know this did not mean ignoring God's commandments to honor their fathers and mothers and care for their children and spouses. Instead, we hear Jesus' invitation to step into the larger family of God, the spacious family that includes every tribe, people, and nation, especially those who are alone. I am amazed by the stories I witness in my community as friends expand their households in creative, life-giving, sometimes even life-saving, ways. God's household is a spacious place for the most vulnerable; Jesus invites families that become households for the least of these (Matthew 25) into unforced rhythms of rest with him.

Spacious friends

Friendship, like family, flourishes in unforced rhythms of freedom and commitment. Spacious friendships are discerned with the same practices that help us discern the spacious path of a Rule of Life—through ordinary practices of humble, prayerful listening and loving, embodied presence. For me, the hardest part of nurturing friendship is the practice of offering consistent embodied presence. I am an introvert and a contemplative. I thrive when I'm given space to think deep thoughts with a lot of pauses built in for reflection. I crave unhurried time to explore the deep and hidden stories in my life and in the lives of others. Sometimes introversion slips into melancholy and inertia, it's true, but that doesn't mean I'm supposed to alter the gifts of my authentic self. It means that I need to live in tender acceptance of who God has made me to be. I need to offer this real, imperfect self—more likely to remember the long-held childhood memory you shared with me than how you take your tea—as an ordinary act of worship to God and ordinary offer of friendship to others. I've come to understand that the kind of friendship I have to offer is a good gift, but it takes some getting used to. Also, it's not for everyone. The good news is that neither is yours. We were all made for perfect friendships, and all of us are still searching.

Years ago, around my thirty-sixth birthday, after months of retreating from hope that I'd ever be able to experience meaningful, sustained friendship, a few good women—women I'd at one time or another set aside in my hunt for the "perfect friend"—invited me to a real-life friendship I did not deserve. After years of frustrating attempts to force rhythms of friendship on ill-fitting relationships, I began to relax in the spacious companionship of faithful friends who were far from perfect, which, I've discovered in the past couple of decades, is the best kind of friend to have.

The little group of imperfect and unlikely friends rescued me out of the relational desert of my mid-thirties and taught me how to be a friend in the most ordinary parts of my life. We spent time together in person weekly, praying, crying, eating, complaining, and laughing. Although time and distance have changed our weekly rhythms, I carry with me the deep inner knowledge of their love. We were a company of friends formed out of pain (sometimes the sort we brought upon each other) and humble origins.

In healing my wounds, Jesus has opened up a spacious path of friendship for me. In spite of many false starts and awkward invitations, I am blessed with an almost embarrassing number of dear friends, other men and women who show up in the pages of my journal, beginning with my friend Lori, who traveled with me on every route of my childhood, high school, and college years and who is returning to me now in a glorious full circle, to the group of friends who gathered this week for a quick Galentine's brunch in the middle of the week, sipping tiny glasses of tiny mimosas because we all had to go back to work in a couple of hours but not before we shared a good laugh and a good cry about the parts of our daily lives that drive us crazy sometimes but also, sometimes, break our hearts.

This is the goodness of God and more than I deserve. It is also the nurturing of each friend along the pathway of my life who held on to me when I was prone to wander into a lonely life overcrowded with my ideal fantasies for friends. Their loving, embodied presence holds space for me to keep showing up as my ordinary, imperfect self. A Rule of Life creates a spacious path, wide enough for my own true self and yours to travel together, grounded in the extraordinary friendship of Jesus, which flourishes in the unforced rhythms of his grace.

Spacious neighbors and neighborhoods

Neighbors and neighborhoods need to take up a lot of real estate on the spacious path and in our Rule of Life. If what Jesus told the law expert in Luke 10 is true, then loving, embodied presence reaches its full potential in our relationships with our neighbors, and in that presence, geography is not insignificant. When Jesus answers the question "Who is my neighbor?" with a story about the good Samaritan, he obliterates the borders of our geographical understanding of the relationship. In Jesus' definition, "neighbor" is larger than those who live next door to us, yet in a spacious Rule of

Life, we can be sure it is never *less* than that definition. Aside from the people who live under our roof, our literal neighbors are the people we have the opportunity to know and love in incredibly practical ways every day of our lives if we choose. Yet often these are the people we know the least.

It might feel that we can't choose our neighbors, but it isn't true. Real estate as an industry commercializes on our desire to choose our neighbors—a desire that, if unchecked, will literally mortgage generations of our family. In the United States, we've euphemized this desire as the "American Dream" and codified it as a system that separates rather than integrates our ability to offer loving, embodied presence in the world. A Rule of Life for spacious neighborhoods invites us to live in a way that powerfully counters our society's ill-fitting systems of housing and land in the transformative and restful way of Jesus.

For over a decade, God has called Brian and me to move into cities where we fall well below the median incomes of property owners. The gift of moving so often and living within financial constraints means we have received the lavish gift of learning all kinds of neighborhoods—neighborhoods we might have only known from a distance had we remained in our hometown where the American Dream of real estate was still within our reach.

What I've learned in this unexpected turn of living arrangements is that an unforced rhythm of presence and proximity is essential to the rule of loving our neighbors as ourselves. When we try to love our neighbors from a distance, we become present to them only from a place of strength. We encounter them on our own terms, with the full strength of our resources and wisdom, and when we cling to the safety of disembodied distance, we don't ever need our neighbors like we think they need us. The rhythms of proximity and presence make space for us to move into the neighborhood as Jesus did with us at his incarnation—which meant more than Nazareth but not less. I've needed the stories of my community[4] to stretch my imagination for neighbors and neighborhoods; the friends and family members who, like Jesus, embrace their own vulnerability and "moved into the neighborhood" (John 1:14, *The Message*) with the vulnerable. A Rule of Life on the spacious path transcends every metric of wealth and invites all of us to rest in God's economy. No matter what zip code we call home, a spacious Rule of Life helps us embody Jesus' loving presence among every kind of vulnerability, even the helplessness of those who—looking for a loophole in God's preference for the least of these—try to squeeze their systems for wealth through the needle's eye of the unforced rhythms of Jesus' gracious kingdom.

BODIES, HEARTS, AND MINDS

When Jesus told the law expert to love God with all his heart, soul, mind, and strength he wasn't speaking in riddles; he was inviting a whole person to wholly love God, others, and himself. The entire person is the self we consider as we discern a Rule of Life. We are one being centered in three parts: body (our physical center), mind (our intellectual center), and heart (our emotional center). Made in the image of the triune God, we are one person with distinct parts. Dallas Willard calls the work of spiritual formation the process of "effectively organizing" all these essential parts of ourselves around God.[5] We hold this in common with each other, and, in the language of the greatest commandment, our tender care for each other and ourselves nurtures our mutual love as an offering of worship to God.

Spacious bodies

Of all the spiritual disciplines, hospitality might be the one that helps us practice best what it means to be a human body. Unfortunately, for many of us, our bodies feel more like unwanted guests. Alternatively, we might treat our body not as a guest but as a dissatisfied tyrant. We see these two postures—rejection and oppression—in the way we treat our own bodies and the bodies around us. Hospitality, however, teaches us to receive, nurture, and provide care for our bodies. Paul assumes this perspective in Ephesians 5 when he says, "No one ever hates his own body, but he nourishes and tenderly cares for it" (NRSVue).

I'm not sure who Paul is thinking about when he writes that verse, but from my perspective, plenty of people hate their own bodies. Unfortunately, the historical church and the ever-evolving Christian marketing subculture have too often appropriated the dominant culture's standard for body size, marketing a faulty theology that suggests God wants your body to look and behave by societal standards. This isn't a modern phenomenon. As long as humans have had bodies, we've been finding ways to mistreat them. Without a healthy theology of the goodness of the body, we don't walk a spacious path. Every other ideal leads away from the restful way of Jesus.

As we consider a Rule of Life, we're not left without some direction from the historical church. Spiritual practices like fasting and feasting form our capacity for contentment, gratitude, moderation, and healthy detachment from disordered desires. Jesus taught us with his body, giving us examples of fasting without self-loathing and feasting without gluttony, working without idolatry, and resting without sloth. He demonstrated the ability to provide for his basic needs with contentment and without envy. In the process of living these rhythms over the years, the Holy Spirit forms our imaginations and develops our muscles (physical and spiritual) in anticipation of our restored and resurrected selves. Other practices for spacious bodies might include prayer walking and other forms of prayerful exercise, healing prayer, holy leisure, medical care, and counseling or behavioral therapy to name the needs and desires of our bodies in a safe place and receive medical treatment as needed.

Only the loving gaze of our Creator is sturdy enough to keep us from falling prey to our culture's shifting ideals. In this light, we can come out of our hiding places and rightly respond with both grateful acceptance and humble conviction to whatever our Creator asks of our bodies. In this response, we participate in the most life-altering kind of acceptance, one that reconciles us with thanksgiving for what God has made, contentment for what God is making, and hope for what God will one day fully restore.

Spacious hearts

When the wisdom writer says, "Keep your heart with all vigilance, for from it flow the springs of life" (Proverbs 4:23 NRSVue), he's talking about tending to this part of us that directs every part of our lives as whole, flourishing human beings. The heart houses our emotions, passions, and desires, and then discloses what we've been storing in our inner selves through our outward actions and habits.

Recalling the etymology for the word *rule* is *regula* might help us imagine a Rule as helping us to nurture a "regulated heart." My son Alex first helped me recognize this connection when I was sharing with him how the root word *regula* best describes the intention of the word *rule* in Rule of Life. "It makes me think what it means to 'self-regulate,'" he said. As a family grateful for various forms of therapeutic care—especially as we listen and learn from my daughter-in-law Rebekah in her training to become a marriage and family therapist—we've become familiar with the practices of self-regulation and the way this kind of care nurtures our overall sense of well-being.

When our emotions become overwhelming or out of control, we call that dysregulation—meaning the emotions no longer help but threaten to harm instead. I don't need to describe to you all the ways we interact with emotional dysregulation in ourselves and the world around us. We can plainly see and name from our own experience that the world has become an emotionally dysregulated place. Our homes have become emotionally dysregulated places. Our hearts are suffering emotional dysregulation at levels we might never have been able to imagine.

A Rule of Life for spacious hearts will include practices that nurture soul care, emotional well-being, and could include retreats, therapeutic and medical care, participation in healing communities, meaningful work, and restful play. In the liturgical seasons, we nurture spacious hearts with silence and celebration, rejoicing and lament. God gave us emotions so that we could know the depth and height and breadth of love. Emotions are a gift to help us experience our inner and outer worlds with nuance and dimension beyond what mere cognitive functions and physical sensations can describe. Whether or not you'd consider yourself a feelings-oriented person, your heart is the place where all your choices and decisions are made and the place from which you offer loving, embodied presence with God, others, and yourself. For this reason, tending to the needs of our emotions and our relationships is essential to discerning a Rule of Life on the spacious path.

Spacious minds

Anxiety disorders affect almost one-fifth of the adult population in the United States—about 48 million people—in any given year.[6] About seventeen million people experience major depressive disorder, seven million people experience bipolar disorder, and nine million people experience post-traumatic stress disorder in the US in any given year.[7] Statistics describe a landscape so vast that I can reasonably assume that one or more of these disorders will make up the local ground that you, reading this book right now, or someone in your family will be walking this year. While medical research for effective treatment for these disorders is beginning to accelerate, a commonly held belief among medical professions is that science has barely scratched the surface of understanding the inner workings of the brain.

All of us—even those who are not suffering effects of acute or chronic mental illness— experience mental fatigue of some kind, never more so than in the wake of navigating the confusing and relentless maze of a global pandemic. Our brains are exhausted and desperately need rest and nourishment. We are experiencing levels of collective weariness that many people describe as unprecedented, yet the long history of the people of God—from Job[8] to Mother Teresa[9] and countless others— reveal stories of people who held together great faith *and* an intimate understanding of deep mental anguish.

Perhaps no saint gives voice to what mental exhaustion and suffering feel like better than David: "Darkness is my closest friend" (Psalm 88:18). David also gives us words for our prayers when our minds are too tired to articulate our own: "How long, O LORD?" (Psalm 13:1–2 NRSVue) and to invite our own selves into prayerful listening: "Why are you cast down, O my soul, and why are you disquieted within me?"

(Psalm 42:5 NRSVue). And when we can't even muster the strength for words, the Holy Spirit "does our praying in and for us, making prayer out of our wordless sighs, our aching groans" (Romans 8:26–27, *The Message*).

A Rule of Life for spacious minds will include practices that nourish peace and foster humble curiosity, that might include liturgical prayer, studying scripture with friends, exploring learning opportunities that are suited to your season of life, reading as rest and reading outside your tradition as hospitality,[10] creative making that refreshes your imagination, healing prayer for anxious patterns of thinking, counseling or therapy to help you examine and name your thoughts in safety and receive medical treatment as needed, and regularly contemplating scripture—especially the Psalms.

In the liturgical seasons, we nurture spacious minds as we slowly and with humble curiosity discover historical and cultural traditions of the church calendar, memorize prayers and scripture (particularly the Psalms), and contemplate the beauty of art and music in the liturgies.

When God commanded us to love God with all our heart, soul, mind, and strength, and to love our neighbors as ourselves, our Creator was inviting us to offer love that engages us at every level—intellect, emotions, physical senses, imagination, and creative energy. And, thanks be to God, a Rule of Life on the spacious path comes to Jesus for physical, emotional, and intellectual rest.

SIX SPHERES: A RULE FOR HOLDING TOGETHER EVERY AREA OF OUR LIFE IN ONE ACT OF WORSHIP

How can a Rule of Life hold together so many categories of our lives—especially when the seasons of our lives are constantly shifting and changing?

Gathering our daily lives around contemplation and community

We might expand the Benedictine focus on prayer, work, study, and hospitality into six spheres or categories of our daily lives. It helps me to imagine these various parts of my life as the six spheres or "petals" that border the inner circle of the Chartres prayer labyrinth.[11] When they get to the center of the laybrinth, prayerful pilgrims often pause to pray in one or more of the six spheres as a kind of a center within the center. So, too, we carry all these distinct—and sometimes conflicting—parts of our true selves into God's one beloved center.

In every sphere of our lives—work and worship, family and friends, body and mind—the rhythms of a Rule of Life on the spacious path help us hold together the story of God with the story of the local ground we travel each day. Once we've understood that a Rule of Life is rooted in Christ, discerned through contemplation and community, and centered in God's beloved community, we can start thinking about the ordinary, everyday practices we want to include in our Rule.

Begin by asking three important questions for each sphere of your life:

1. What are you noticing as your default Rule of Life for this sphere?
2. How could your community help you listen and respond to Jesus' invitations in this sphere of your life?
3. How does Sabbath rest fit in this sphere of my life?

After reflecting on these three questions, select which area of your life you are most drawn to begin your Rule of Life. Reflect on the questions specific to that sphere.

Spiritual: The practices that Jesus invites us to keep that nurture prayer, scripture reading, and embodied worship.

- When will you pray? With whom? Is there a particular expression of prayer that feels most inviting to you right now?
- When will you read scripture and what method seems most inviting for this season of your life?
- Who might you invite to listen to you as you discern the movements of God in your life? Who might God be inviting you to offer the same listening?
- Which local congregation is God inviting you to embrace by saying yes to stability and change?

Relational: The practices that Jesus invites us to keep to nurture the people we encounter during the everyday work and worship of our real lives.

- As you consider the examples I've shared to describe spacious family, friends, and neighbors, what ordinary rhythms are you already keeping? What feels unforced and restful? What feels forced and burdensome?
- How do your relational rhythms fit within your season of life? Are you sensing a need to update or adapt your practices to better match the relational rhythms in your life right now?
- In what way will you love and receive love in the relationships on the everyday routes of your life? What practices will help you tend that love? In what way does a spacious path invite you to expand your everyday routes to give and receive love from "the least of these" (Matthew 25)?

Intellectual and Emotional: The practices that Jesus invites us to keep to nourish our hearts and minds as an act of worship.

- What ordinary rhythms are you already keeping that nurture your mind and heart? What feels unforced and restful? What feels forced and burdensome?
- What kind of care might you need to tend to your mind and heart? How might that care fit within this season of life?
- As you browse the potential practices that nurture a spacious mind and heart, what sound most inviting to you? How would that practice fit within the ordinary days of your life right now?

Physical: The practices that Jesus invites us to keep that care for and nourish our bodies as an act of worship.

- What ordinary rhythms are you already keeping that nurture your body? What feels unforced and restful? What feels forced and burdensome?
- What kind of care might you need to tend to your body? How might that care fit within this season of life?
- As you browse the potential practices that nurture a spacious body, what sound most inviting to you? How would that practice fit within the ordinary days of your life right now?

Financial: The practices that Jesus invites us to keep, giving our resources in the way he invited the rich young ruler.

- In what way does a spacious path invite you to expand your everyday finances to give and receive love from "the least of these" (Matthew 25)?
- How has the vision of the American Dream informed the financial systems you follow?
- How do the rhythms of spacious work (and spacious hospitality in the next chapter) shape your imagination for keeping your finances in God's Sabbath economy? What rhythms are you already keeping? What feels unforced and restful? What feels forced and burdensome?

Missional: The practices that Jesus invites us to keep that help us love our neighbors as ourselves as an act of worship.

- In what way will you love the vulnerable in the relationships on the everyday routes of your life? What practices will help you tend that love?
- In what way does a spacious path invite you to expand your everyday routes to give and receive love from "the least of these" (Matthew 25)?
- How do the rhythms of spacious work (and spacious hospitality in the next chapter) shape your imagination for the work Jesus is inviting to join him in? What ordinary rhythms are you already keeping? What feels unforced and restful? What feels forced and burdensome?

KEEPING A RULE OF LIFE ON THE SPACIOUS PATH

The earth is the LORD's and all that is in it, the world, and those who live in it.

—PSALM 24:1 (NRSVUE)

Read Colossians 1:15–20 or Romans 12:1–2 through slowly and, if possible, out loud a couple of times. What word or phrase catches your attention? How does your body feel as you read Paul's words about Jesus holding all things together? What questions come to mind? What do you need help with to say yes to Jesus' invitation? Could you put that need into a one-sentence prayer for help?

FOR FURTHER REFLECTION

1. How would you begin to describe the landscape of your life right now? What resonated with you as you read the findings from recent surveys about fragmented work and family relationships?
2. How might this sentence inform your practice of a Rule of Life? "Reality . . . is always our trustworthy, supportive friend. God lives and moves and has his

being in that which is real. Because God dwells in
reality, our relationship with him can only happen
there."[1]

3. At first glance and without analyzing your answers,
   which of the statements about spacious work are you
   most drawn to? Which are you least drawn to?

4. In what ways do you practice Sabbath? What art or
   activity draws you toward Sabbath rest?

5. Chapter 10, "Ordinary and (Extraordinary) Time,"
   invites us to consider the tensions inherent to changing seasons. How have you experienced a connection
   between change and rest? How would you begin to
   name your current season of life?

6. As you think about the seven liturgical seasons,
   which feel most inviting to consider? Where do you
   feel some resistance? Why might that be?

7. As you read the descriptions of the "six spheres" in
   chapter 11, what feels inviting to you in your life
   right now? What feels incompatible with your life
   right now?

8. As you continue to notice the everyday pattern of
   your life with gentle curiosity rather than reflexive
   judgment, what experiences or practices from this
   section feel most inviting to your Rule of Life? Share
   your response with a trusted friend. Ask them to
   simply pray for you.

FURTHER PRACTICES FOR CONTEMPLATION AND COMMUNITY: PRAYER WALKING AND SABBATH

Understanding the gift of God's presence in the reality of my
ordinary life helps me say yes to Jesus' invitation to spacious

work. Here are a couple of practices that have become essential to keeping my Rule of Life on a spacious path.

Prayer walking

Prayer walking is defined as "a way of saturating a particular place and people with prayer. This discipline draws us out of prayers that are limited to our immediate concerns and into a larger circle of God's loving attention."[2] You might choose the neighborhood surrounding your home, church, or workplace. You can walk alone or with others. In every case, remember that you are in the company of the triune God and God's beloved communion of saints.

There are no set prayers for this discipline. You can pray whatever comes to your heart and mind as you pass various homes, parks, and places of business. You might match your breath and pace to the beautiful Aaronic blessing that begins "The Lord bless you and keep you" (Numbers 6:24–26). Another suggestion is to alternate specific biblical phrases like "Come, Lord Jesus," and "Mercy triumphs over judgment" (James 2:13). The Lord's Prayer offers a beautiful, substantive template for a prayer walk. If nothing else, consider the phrase "May your kingdom come, on earth as it is in heaven" as you walk your neighborhood.

Post-walk reflection
- What prayer most resonated as you walked?
- What did you notice as you prayed that you had not noticed before?
- What prayers do you feel particularly compelled to continue praying?

Sabbath

Keeping the Sabbath is a practice saturated with historical and theological meaning, yet the actual practice doesn't
need to be complicated. As an invitation to cease doing and
embrace being, keeping the Sabbath will help us reorient our
entire week in the direction of Jesus, others, and ourselves. It's
a simple practice, but so countercultural to the forced rhythms
of productivity and frenetic recreation that it may be one of
the hardest spiritual disciplines we ever attempt. Maybe it
helps to think of it in terms of fasting and feasting; we fast
from productive work to feast on holy leisure.

As Christians, most of us will keep Sundays as our Sabbath day and build our rhythms for rest and feasting around
gathering for worship with our church families. For some of
us, Sundays require essential work, and we'll need to be creative about what day to practice Sabbath. Because Brian is a
pastor, we have found the Jewish tradition of time beginning
with evening helpful here. We often practice a Sabbath day
from Thursday at 6 p.m. to Friday at 6 p.m. If you are uncertain whether the work you find yourself doing on Sundays is
"essential work," invite your community to help you discern
how Jesus is inviting you to keep the Sabbath.

Even after years of practice, I have learned that Sabbath
almost never happens by accident. Resting requires intention-
ality, not unlike the Jewish customs of preparing their entire
household in advance of *shabbat*. Adele Calhoun recommends
planning for a "twenty-four-hour Sabbath you can enter with
anticipation" by beginning "gently on the evening before."[3]
She recommends simple rituals that signal rest to our minds
and bodies: light a candle, go to bed early, share your hopes
for the next day with friends and family, and ask God to guide
you throughout the coming day.

Prepare for a full day to cease doing to embrace being, by considering what habits nurture rest and what habits require work. Adele Calhoun recommends considering "the things that would nourish you" and "plan them spaciously into the day"[4]: worship, music, a nap, making art, walking, reading, playing with children, a delicious dessert, or feasting with friends. In addition, consider the things that would tax you: emails, social media, shopping, problem solving, difficult conversations, or work deadlines. Remove those expectations from your day.

As I have returned again and again to a Rule of Life for Sabbath-keeping, I choose again and again to believe that there is a way of Christian rest, the restful way of Jesus. I believe the Christ who naps in capsizing boats follows the footsteps of his Father who takes days off even though the spinning universe depends on God's attention. God works and God rests. Jesus is the rest of God given to us; He is Lord Rest.

Lord of the Sabbath, help us rest with you. Amen.

PART 4

Blessing a Rule of Life on the Spacious Path

A rule that makes space to bless the challenges that upend our lives as the creative tensions of God's kingdom

Prepare for Part 4 by reading Matthew 19:20–22 and Matthew 5:1–12

Sometimes the invitations of Jesus feel like heart-breaking tension before they feel like unforced rhythms of grace. Sometimes we feel the tensions dissipate as we mature in Christ and into our true selves. Sometimes the tensions we feel are the result of the objective realities of living in a fallen world. Death is a tension we will continue to experience until Jesus returns, yet we face that tension with the knowledge that death is ultimately defeated. We live between the fall and the final resurrection when all things will be restored to life. This tension doesn't exist as a rabbit trail along the spacious path; the spacious path makes room for blessing the tensions in our lives and in the world.

One of the most disorienting moments of walking a prayer labyrinth occurs when the path turns 180 degrees from the center. People who design and build labyrinths call these places the "turns" of the circuits, and as a symbol for walking the journey of life, the turns pack a punch of meaning. In theological terms, when we hear the word "turn," we might think of every prophet's favorite word in scripture: "Repent!" We know this to mean *Turn around! Go the other direction! This way is leading you away from God's commands!*

The turns in a prayer labyrinth as symbol for being open to repentance are deeply meaningful, and a Rule of Life as a spacious path makes room for us to turn around in repentance as well. When we consistently exercise humble, prayerful listening and loving, embodied presence to discern the invitations of Jesus, we will find that repentance, like obedience, surprisingly leads us to rest. The prophet Isaiah may as well be describing the law expert's response to Jesus' invitation to sell all that he had and follow him:

> This is what the Sovereign Lord, the Holy One of
> Israel, says:
> "In repentance and rest is your salvation,
>   in quietness and trust is your strength,
>   but you would have none of it." (Isaiah 30:15)

Repentance—initiated by God's kindness (Romans 2:4)—leads us to rest, and in the coming pages, we'll explore that paradox. I'd like to consider an additional meaning for the turns in a prayer labyrinth, one evoked by the intricate artistic design woven into the circular geometric pattern. The Chartres labyrinth in France, for example, includes twenty-eight 180-degree turns, each with a rounded edge. Traditionally, these back-to-back turns are shaped like bow ties, also called *labryses*.[1] Labyrinth designers offer the option of making this connection with a straight line, but for those who'd like to get fancier, there's the option of rounding the turns, which of course the Chartres designers did. The result is that, with a Christian imagination, the *labryses* look like small chalices. Pilgrims who walk the Chartres labyrinth pass by a chalice-shaped symbol ten times. Ten times, prayerful pilgrims are invited to recall that the path that follows Jesus comes with the question, "Can you drink this cup?" (Matthew 20:17–28).

When Jesus asked the disciples this question, he followed up with a promise: "You will drink this cup, but I will drink it first." He reminds them again of the principles of God's new kingdom reality, where the least are the greatest and the masters are the servants of all. Earlier in Matthew he had eloquently preached the sermon we all keep reading centuries later, the sermon of God's economy where those of us who are at the end of our rope find ourselves holding on to a rope that never runs out. Not only that, but we also find that instead of merely surviving, the spacious path blesses all the unexpected, painful, upending turns of our lives to makes us more like Jesus and more like the beloved selves God has always imagined.

In the coming chapters, we'll consider how the incredible reality that Jesus became one of us influences how we shape a Rule of Life. We'll listen for and respond to the invitation to begin a Rule of Life that, rather than attempting to map a trajectory of continual forward movement toward a forced spiritual maturity, instead makes space for us to live fully beloved and blessed like Jesus—who intimately understands the tension of being human in a fragmented world. As a method for blessing the tensions that threaten to upend our lives, a Rule of Life helps us envision the practices of God's kingdom— hospitality, lament, sacrificial generosity, biblical justice, and more—all the while keeping company with the gentle and humble Jesus who promises to give us rest even in the middle of our deepest pain and disappointment. Rather than being a road that leads to nowhere, suffering in God's kingdom is the way of a spacious path where Jesus himself keeps us company.

CHAPTER 12

KEEP COMPANY WITH ME

Saying Yes to Spacious Hospitality

It's not about offering a show place; it's about offering a safe place.
—MY MOM, NANCY G. HILL[1]

Hospitality is another one of those Christian words we reference often, yet understand only a little. For years, I assumed hospitality was the habit of having people over to the house and serving them a nice meal. My mother and grandmother excelled in this kind of hospitality, and I eagerly followed all the things they'd taught me. Yet hospitality, like rule, means so much more than this one thing. We hear the dimensions of spacious hospitality in the many English words we use from this one root word, *hospitalitas*, including hospital, hotel, hospice, and host. I've read that the Greek word for hospitality, *philoxenia,* means love of foreigners or strangers and that the root word *Xenos* or *hospes* can mean three things: stranger, guest, *and* host. The interchanging roles of hospitality are embedded in the roots of the word. As in the life of Jesus, we see the rhythm of hospitality as moving with each other in the giving and receiving of hospitality.

Hospitality motivates every act of loving presence we give and receive. In terms of a Rule of Life as a spacious path, I'm inviting us to especially imagine hospitality as a commitment to loving the vulnerable. The command to love the "other" saturates the entire Bible, and the terms are not vague. When God tells us to love the "other," scripture tells us exactly who that means we should love: the stranger, foreigner, prisoner, and outcast.

Thankfully, my parents taught me a lot about this kind of hospitality, too.

LOVING STRANGERS

In August 2021, we celebrated my mother's retirement. For fifty years, she served as a teacher in all kinds of settings. For the last dozen years of her career, she poured her heart and soul into her students who had arrived in her small town from all over the globe and were learning English as an additional language. She taught them to read and love language the way she taught in every context—with creativity, passion, and love.

The year before she began her job at the civic association in our hometown, an angry former student barricaded the building and killed fourteen people, including teachers.[2] Still, my mom took the job because she loves language and teaching and has grown to love the image of God represented in all peoples. She learned how to teach English in every creative way possible to a classroom that spoke dozens of different languages, except English. She taught through masks, face shields, and severe back pain for the last couple of years. And her students loved her.

At her retirement dinner, she began sharing stories from her final months of work. She told us about the two women from Colombia in one of her classes who took her out for farewell margaritas (my mother's first), which became her favorite beverage. She told us about an older couple from Korea and a woman from Turkey who gathered for dinner at my parents' house. Mom ordered pizza, and the Muslim woman graciously removed the pepperoni and then, out of her deep gratitude, insisted on hand-washing the dinner dishes. After dinner, my parents modeled the hanbok they wore when my brother married my sister-in-law a couple of decades ago. The Korean couple said they would like to be my parents' neighbors.

Just two stories of strangers becoming friends, and she has so many more.

Her students called her Teacher Nancy, and at her retirement dinner, we celebrated her steady, faithful work on behalf of people most of us could consider "the other." My mom used the blessing God gave her to bless countless others; in the process, we, her family, were blessed.

HOSPITALITAS

Professor and writer Christine Pohl says that the dimensions of our hospitality are shaped by the "wideness of God's mercy and the generosity of God's welcome."[3] The monastic rule for hospitality takes this boundless measure of God's hospitality seriously, receiving every guest as if they *were* Christ. From my experience in the Irish monastery, I know that sometimes monks aren't especially warm in their hospitality. Father Donovan welcomed us, kind of like the monk in the old monastic legend who, seeing in the distance yet another guest entering the monastery grounds, mutters under his breath, "Oh, Christ, is that you again?" In response to God's abundance, we are continually enlarging our borders and sharing more of our resources; we give with what we've been given—everything— to the Christ who comes again and again and again.

It's no small fact that the development of hospitals in the late fourth century coincides with the monastic movement of the same time. As Christians gathered inward in monastic contemplation, their prayer became an embodied, healing presence to the sick and dying around them.

In his rule, Benedict writes, "All guests to the monastery shall be welcomed as Christ because he will say, 'I was a stranger, and you took me in.'"[4] *Hospitalitas* in the Benedictine tradition is a radical hospitality, but no more radical than what Jesus demonstrates in his life. One of my favorite observations about how Jesus demonstrates hospitality is that we see him *receive* hospitality almost as often as we see him *offer* hospitality (maybe even more). In this way, our definition of spacious hospitality expands from the perspective of a patron or benefactor to the with-ness Jesus lives with others. In Jesus' restful way, hospitality becomes a way to welcome and be welcomed, to give and receive care, to be merciful and receive mercy.

SPACIOUS HOSPITALITY

What spacious hospitality is and what spacious hospitality is not

Saying yes to spacious hospitality involves vulnerability and risk. Rather than looking for Christ in each stranger, we train our eyes to see Christ *between* us and all strangers. We trust that in loving Christ, our love for the stranger will be put to good ends even when the love we give is not returned or, worse, when the love we share is exploited. That is why this spacious offer of hospitality requires the wisdom and safekeeping of the community.

Saying yes to spacious hospitality nurtures the welcoming presence we desire for all of our relationships. We recognize

that parenting is hospitality, friendship is hospitality, our inter-
actions at work and with our neighbors are acts of hospitality,
and how we care for ourselves is an act of hospitality.

Saying yes to spacious hospitality energizes our humble,
prayerful listening to God, others, and ourselves. When we
listen to another person's story—without interruption or
agenda—we offer a profound act of hospitality. When we
mourn with those who are weeping and rejoice with those
who are celebrating, we keep company with Jesus and others.

We keep company with Jesus when we love our enemies and
forgive those who have wronged us. We keep company with
Jesus when we offer embodied presence to the outcast and the
lonely. Even more radically, we receive hospitality in the places
where the poor and the sick and prisoners and the lonely dwell.
This is what it means to say yes to spacious hospitality.

Jesus never intended for us to walk through the earth as private benefactors, operating from our capacity to discern who
deserves our hospitality and who doesn't. Personal hospitality
is a limited, finite resource. On our own, we can meet some
needs and welcome some strangers. This is not meaningless,
but it is fixed. When we expand our vision to the hospitality we
offer as a community, we find abundance rather than scarcity.

In a stunning act of abundant hospitality, our Jewish neighbors made a home for our homeless Anglican church within
the walls of their synagogue. Making room for us in their
cherished worship space would be loving on its own, but what
they have offered us and what we have reciprocated is a loving, embodied presence. Unexpectedly, we have become each
other's community in demonstrating love to the neighborhood.
When one congregation collects supplies to offer Afghan refugees, the other congregation joins in. In the winter, when our
congregation wraps a Christmas tree with mittens and scarves

collected for the nearby city mission, Congregation Rodeph Sholom adds to the tree with us.

We also participate in each other's celebrations and suffering. During Sukkot, our children craft paper chains to decorate the booth behind the synagogue, and during Hanukkah, we hold hands and dance in a circle together. On Twelfth Night, they come to our party and sing carols with us. When Brian bakes the round loaves of bread he serves our congregation for eucharist, he adds honey from the jar our Jewish neighbors gave us during Rosh Hashanah. On Yom HaShoah, we all light candles remembering the Jewish people who were murdered at the hands of the Nazis during the Holocaust of World War II.

We go to church on Sundays after our Jewish friends worshiped on Saturday in a building protected by police and security guards. When anti-Semitism rears its evil head, we hope our Jewish neighbors feel buffered by our presence. When our impoverished city's homeless and hopeless citizens wander into the courtyard from the streets, they do not care if a Jew or a Gentile greets them. They encounter the reality of community as a loving, embodied presence in their neighborhood. A Rule of Life provides a spacious path for giving and receiving love with a community of those we consider culturally or religiously "other" from ourselves.

Together, we receive the spacious hospitality of God, and together, we extend it.

CHAPTER 13

CRUCIFORM LOVE

What would happen to our faith if we believed that God reigns sovereign over both our celebration and our suffering?

—SOONG-CHAN RAH[1]

What is the purpose of lament? It allows us to connect with and grieve the reality of our sin and suffering. It draws us to repentant connection with God in that suffering. Lament also serves as an effort to change God's mind, to ask him to turn things around in our favor. Lament seeks God as comforter, healer, restorer, and redeemer. Somehow the act of lament reconnects us with God and leads us to hope and redemption.

—LATASHA MORRISON[2]

If the restful way of Jesus finds its footing between the borderlines of contemplation and community, then loving the vulnerable makes those footprints stick to the path. Indeed, this is the only path to walk if we wish to follow Jesus. We don't know the religious scholar's motives when he asked Jesus what he needed to do to gain eternal life, but it seems like Jesus makes space for an open exchange as he invites conversation about God's laws and then brilliantly summarizes them in two commands: love God and love your neighbor as yourself. Matthew's gospel account shows that this does little to faze the rich man, who believes he has accomplished those commandments and does not yet distrust his own sincerity in questioning Jesus. In the middle of this exchange, between the law expert's love for rules and Jesus' rule for love, we read this astounding sentence in Mark 10:21: "Jesus looked him hard in the eye—and loved him!" (*The Message*). Out of love, Jesus invites the man to a loving act of obedience: "If you want to give it all you've got," Jesus replied, "go sell your possessions; give everything to the poor. All your wealth will then be in heaven. Then come follow me" (my paraphrase).

When faced with Christ's words on money and possessions, it's tempting to do exegetical backflips to make the verses mean something other than money and possessions. Whenever scripture focuses on wealth, it may be referring to more than money and possessions, but it never means less; God's kingdom economy and Jesus' teaching about money form the foundation for biblical justice. In this encounter, we might at least respect the rich young man for knowing the difference between what Jesus was commanding and what he was willing to do. He knew his wealth mattered more to him than following Jesus, and it broke his heart but didn't change his life.

In the Luke 10 version of this encounter between Jesus and the law expert, the young man tries to find a semantic loophole to squeeze through about the definitions of neighbors. Jesus responds with the story of the Good Samaritan. Matthew's account tells us that this is the point when the man finally recognizes his shortcomings: "That was the last thing the young man expected to hear. And so, crestfallen, he walked away. He was holding on tight to a lot of things, and he couldn't bear to let go" (Matthew 19:22, *The Message*). Somewhere in between giving away his wealth and loving all people, especially the vulnerable, as his neighbors, the lover of the law walked away from Jesus' invitation to keep company with him.

SPACIOUS REPENTANCE

There are no shortcuts around suffering on the spacious path, but there is always companionship. In a poem about agape love, the Apostle Paul helps us imagine the kind of love Jesus invites in Luke 10—the kind of love that costs everything. Theologian Fleming Rutledge refers to this powerful vision, writing that "over against all that the world calls 'love,'" the true nature of Christian love can only be seen from the perspective of the crucifixion.[2] If we believe this to be true (and I do), then we understand that we can't "virtue signal" cruciform love; we must be transformed by faithful, embodied agape love.

We embody cruciform love when we embrace both suffering and resurrection. Lament articulates the full dialect of love and trains us to speak the same language as the Christ we hear uttering anguish from the cross and the Christ we hear speaking peace to Mary weeping near the open tomb. On his way to the cross, Christ invites all of us who are weary and burnt out on artificial demonstrations of sorrow to bear up under the weight of love with him. When we practice the agape of Christ's passion, a Rule of Life will make space for us to embody Christ's resurrection peace in the world.

In the summer of 2020, my friend and fellow spiritual director Vernée Wilkinson spoke at a series of retreats I was leading entitled "Spiritual Practices for Living as an Antiracist Person." The idea for the retreats began earlier that summer when Vernée and Ted Wuest, a faculty member from the organization where we received our training, collaborated to translate the examen, an ancient contemplative prayer from Saint

Ignatius, into a real-time examination of conscience for white Christians. Vernée sent the prayer, entitled "A Daily Examen for Living as an Antiracist Person," to our spiritual direction colleagues three weeks after George Floyd, a forty-six-year-old Black man was murdered by a white police officer in Minneapolis, Minnesota; and three months after Breonna Taylor, a twenty-six-year-old Black woman was fatally shot when seven police officers entered her Louisville, Kentucky, apartment; and four months after Ahmaud Arbery, a twenty-five-year-old Black man was murdered during a racially motivated hate crime in Brunswick, Georgia.

The small group of mostly white women who participated in the retreat series committed to praying the daily examen Vernée had written and then meeting virtually three times throughout the summer to sit together in silence and lament. Each time we met, Vernée joined our video call for about a half hour to generously offer us her lived experience as a Black woman. During one of our conversations, I asked Vernée if listening, learning, lamenting, and living differently happen in a chronological order. She responded that while the recent headlines were prompting a lot of white communities to say, "We're *really* listening now," speaking for herself as a Black woman, "it's been hard to hear that because historically and personally, there's been plenty of accounts on the record that have been wildly inappropriate . . . and not that different from what George Floyd experienced." She went on to say:

> Listening can be done while accountability is being taken, while forward action is being taken, and also while understanding that it's not necessarily going to be perfect work and having the humility that there might be some missteps in your work of being an antiracist person . . . don't let that

stop the work. . . . This is about a work of justice and we serve a just God so it's a little bit too easy to get caught in the feelings and attempt toward perfection. To do antiracist work, there has to be room for error, and just trusting we can continue to work through it together.[4]

As I listened to Vernée, I began to understand a more holistic perspective for repentance—one that makes space for listening, lamenting, learning, and living differently all at the same time. In God's mercy and in the restful way of Jesus, repentance turns us around, and reorients us in the direction of the vulnerable.

In a spacious Rule of Life, listening can never fully bring about the work of repentance, but it's an important piece of entering that work. The same spirit that empowers us to listen as an act of repentance will initiate and empower us—in community and strengthened by the never-depleted power of the Holy Spirit—to do the work of justice.

SEVEN WORDS: A RULE FOR HOLDING TOGETHER CROSS AND RESURRECTION

How might Jesus' life and teaching help us find rest in repentance and lament? How do lament and repentance make room for spacious hospitality?

Practice Lament

While suffering and grief have always been a part of the human condition, the customs we enact to express lament have dwindled in a sentimental and stoic world. Practicing lament, without guidance, might as well be a recommendation to begin speaking to each other in Latin. In a world bearing witness to continual violence, idioms like "sending thoughts and prayers" sound inadequate, if not ridiculous, but what words and actions offer rest for the fatigue of our unre-solved grief?

Somewhere during the decade of my thirties—those years God was leading me through significant and often painful growth toward healing and wholeness—I realized I needed a sturdier foundation for all the grief I saw in my own life and in the lives of people around me. Then in 2012, during our first Holy Week in Austin, we attended our church's Good Friday service, arranged around Jesus' last words on the cross before he died. Seven members of the congregation responded to one of Jesus' last words with their own story of suffering. I felt like

THE SEVEN WORDS

"Father, forgive them, for they do not know what they are doing." (Luke 23:34)

"Truly I tell you, today you will be with me in paradise." (Luke 23:43)

"Here is your mother." (John 19:27)

"My God, my God, why have you forsaken me?" (Matthew 27:46; Mark 15:34)

"I am thirsty." (John 19:28)

"It is finished." (John 19:30)

"Father, into your hands I commit my spirit." (Luke 23:46)

I'd finally found a way to both adore Christ and acknowledge the lament of suffering in one communal act of worship. I've come to rely on this practice to prepare me for a more full-throated resurrection celebration every Easter.

Each Holy Week since then, following the example of our church in Austin, I've published a series of lament stories written by friends and colleagues to help us walk with Christ toward the cross. The guest writers tell stories of walking with Jesus on paths of suffering that include every sort of grief: illness, relational disillusionment, anxiety, joblessness, death of loved ones, and the death of dearly held dreams. Their stories have helped form my understanding of cruciform suffering.[5] Along the way I've come to rely on a community who can sit with me in my grief rather than try to persuade me out of it. This became the sort of value that defined my relationships—those who welcomed me into their own suffering and shared mine became my dearest friends.

The holy compulsion motivating the Holy Week lament series contends for this truth: We need to hear other people's laments in the presence of Christ and his people. Specifically, we need to hear stories outside our own perspective and from all different stages of grief. I need to hear expressions of lament at the beginning, shocking part of grief, the middle, uncharted terrain of grief, and the lament that comes with the ending chapters of grief. I need to be surrounded by people who aren't afraid to share their lament in all its unpredictability and strength.

Now, in our church in Connecticut, we invite lament in through particular practices[6] and prayers all year round, culminating in the same Good Friday liturgy we learned in Austin. We are also learning that spacious lament makes room for spacious celebration.

PRACTICE RESURRECTION

One year, after attending Good Friday service together, my daughters and I talked honestly about how sometimes Eastertide can feel like a let-down. It seems to be easier to understand fasting better than feasting. We thought that might be, in part, because our world is generally obsessed with feasting, and whatever we try to do to mark Eastertide feels like the stuff we're normally trying to do every day anyway.

I wonder, too, if sometimes feasting shows more plainly how far away from God we still live. When I can be satisfied with just the right amount of wine or chocolate, that is feasting. When I can't stop either one, that turns into gluttony which is no longer true feasting. In some ways, fasting is easier, yes?

Put another way: feasting is a discipline, too. We take in the good with gratitude and contentment without making an idol of the gifts. This requires us to depend on the Creator as much as (maybe more than) any other spiritual exercise.

During Lent, we walk with Jesus toward the cross. During Easter, we walk with the first disciples away from the grave and toward the realization that death has had its last day and that the resurrection power of Jesus reigns. The rhythms of a Rule of Life help me keep watching and learning from Jesus and others the balance between activism and rest, love of neighbor and self, and lament and rejoicing. Bent in the shape of Jesus' cruciform love, we participate in God's works of justice and peace in the world.

CHAPTER 14

BLESSING THE END
OF THE ROAD

And now the words that sweep down the years like a wind that
sometimes grinds the soul with the teeth of winter and at other
times heal it with the scented oils of spring. A paradox and more
than that. Discovering our poverty we find that we are already rich,
in letting go of everything we get the best of it all back, heaped up
and overflowing, the staggering bounty that is the inheritance of the
true believer.

— EUGENE C. KENNEDY[1]

The expected and unexpected, common and chaotic, planned
and unpredictable turns of our lives are held together in
one journey of seeking God. The beauty of the spacious path
is that there are no dead ends, and we aren't left to map out
our lives by our own intelligence, self-discipline, or sheer good
luck. We aren't even responsible for finding a grand scheme we
might label as "God's will for our one life." We are invited to
seek God. Even then, we discover that more faithful than our
seeking is God's commitment to finding us, and more faithful
than our welcoming the vulnerable is God's commitment to
welcoming us.

HE WANTS US TO BE NOTHING

In spring 2020 I tacked a hand-scribbled index card to the wall over my desk. In uneven ink, the handwriting directs me: "Learn to articulate your outrage. April 16, 2020." I'd written the statement—a direct quote from author Marilyn McEntyre[2]—on a day when the exhaustion of chronic indignation felt fearfully close to hatred. Earlier that day, during a conversation with my spiritual director, that word, *hatred*, slipped out of my mouth as a confession. It shocked me. As I sat in silence with my hatred and the loving presence of my spiritual director, I remembered the advice and wrote it on the three-by-five card as a prayer: *Learn to articulate your outrage. Amen.*

In April 2020 the whole world was getting a crash course in infectious disease. My grandmother died in March, and we were forced to ask the same question that families of millions would face in 2020: How do we grieve when we can't be together? At the same time, I was googling "How to postpone a wedding because of the pandemic." My daughter's April 25th celebration could not happen as planned, and we added another layer of unexpected grief (who expects to postpone a wedding?) formed by the question: How do we celebrate when we can't be together?

Then in May 2020, a 12:30 a.m. phone call triggered a frantic drive to the airport and a flight across the country in the middle of a pandemic so that we could stand outside a psychiatric hospital to show our loved one we were there. We could not hug her, but she could see our faces and we could see hers—at least the outline of her beautiful curly hair, three stories up, silhouetted by the glare of late-spring Texas sun. She was alive, and we needed to see it with our own eyes.

The spiritual practice of a Rule of Life has helped me keep moving in the direction of Jesus through all kinds of societal and personal disruption—financial strain, multiple moves, caring for family members suffering acute illness, starting a new job, hosting my children's weddings, and becoming a grandparent, to name a few things. A Rule of Life helps me map the practices of listening and love that route and reroute me through the ubiquitous detours of my days. They help me orient my life in the restful way of Jesus. Through long seasons of unemployment and underemployment, through other seasons of financial strain, relational heartbreak, flooded basements, and emergency surgeries, I've felt the tensions of life like a sucking force of gravity, when it felt like my legs couldn't hold me any longer—literally and figuratively.

Perhaps no other pressure has flattened me more often than mental illness—my own and in those I love. During one particularly painful season, as we cared for one of our children during a mental health crisis, Brian and I both took a leave of absence from our work. We fell on the mercy of God and our community to help us bridge the gap of what we had to leave undone, and most days were able to live from that mercy. On other days, the mercy felt depleted. Used up. Beyond reach.

Like all grief, the kind our family has experienced is not something we can schedule. It comes in waves—sometimes chronic and dull like a toothache and other times pain that is acute and searing. One morning, in the middle of the worst part of the leave of absence, I woke in a daze and headed toward the kitchen for coffee. I got as far as the dining room table and felt like I couldn't take one more step. The kitchen felt too far away. I sank down to the floor and leaned against the table legs. I don't know why I picked that spot, but it's where I landed; in hindsight, I suspect it felt like a kind of shelter for my weary head. I tried to pray. About fifteen minutes later, Brian found me in this position and sat down next to me, not speaking, just waiting for an explanation for this surprising place I'd landed. All I knew to explain my posture was, "It feels like God wants us to be nothing."

My lament beneath the dining room table felt like an unbearable tension, but as I spoke the words, I noticed myself feeling lighter. "God wants us to be nothing," began to feel like a blessing rather than a curse. In the months and years since then, including the last few years of deep suffering and grief we've all been living, we have returned to this statement again and again as an odd reassurance: "God wants us to be nothing." As we've continued to practice humble, prayerful listening and loving, embodied presence within community, we've heard Jesus add to our prayer: "I am your everything." So now we say to each other, when we need to be reminded, "God wants us to be nothing so God can give us Jesus, who is our everything."

Anger is the stage of grief I got stuck in for most of 2020. My friends and children seemed to ricochet between denial and depression. Folks in the congregations we know demonstrated a solid penchant for bargaining and a few people embodied a peace-filled acceptance. I, however, was enraged. Occasionally I stomped around my house, yelling prayers to God. Other times, I privately cursed the most mundane inconveniences. I needed to find a way to articulate the outrage rather than be ground up in a wake of unsatisfactory social media outbursts or sulky episodes of self-loathing. I needed to get a good night's sleep.

Yet, I learned that even outrage felt better than feeling nothing. "Nothing" is a disorienting absence of feeling, and notably, nothing sometimes feels like we're on a path leading nowhere. Not being able to perceive God's presence or to sense our place within God's beloved community can feel small, cramped, dark, and maybe even like a dead end. That is how I felt sitting underneath the dining room table: *I cannot go further. I have reached a dead end.* I imagine you have your own version of this kind of moment. Maybe you're sitting in one right now, with your face pressed up against the wall of nowhere to turn. I wish I could give you a hug or stomp around my house and yell prayers on your behalf. Would you take my encouragement instead? The restful way of Jesus does not bypass or reroute around suffering. The spacious path has no dead ends. This is not a dead end, it's a place to pause, even to collapse, if needed. It's a place to lean into the borders of contemplation and community until you can see the next step.

As I look back on that season of intense suffering, the most fruitful expressions of anger took the form of embodied gestures—nine of us sitting in an empty sanctuary to watch my daughter and new son-in-law say vows in April, and then twenty of us, masked and six feet apart, circling my grandparents' caskets at a delayed burial service in early June. The next week, we wore those same masks to kneel in the grass of our neighborhood park for eight minutes and forty-six seconds with our community, silently cursing systems of oppression complicit with the murder of George Floyd. In May, we stood with our sons and daughter-in-law outside the psychiatric hospital and protested death by lifting a heart-shaped balloon into the sky outside our loved one's hospital window. In November, I added a visual to my thumb-tacked index card. Next to the sentence "Learn to articulate your outrage" I placed the sticker I proudly earned. It says, "I Voted."

Through all the personal and global suffering of that year, I needed the anger I was feeling to be transformed into a cleansing, redemptive grief. I needed humble, prayerful listening and loving, embodied presence to help me discern fruitful practices to articulate my outrage and to sit with my grief. While that year, which took extraordinary global suffering and mashed it into the ground of some extraordinary suffering in our personal lives, is thankfully not a typical level of suffering for us, the disciplines we'd been practicing did help us navigate a new (ab)normal.

THE LUCKY-ARE-THEYS

Years ago, my husband and I had the privilege of hearing Eugene Peterson speak at a symposium about forming a Christian imagination for blessing and creating culture.[3] Peterson explained how his years of pastoring congregations were formative in his approach to paraphrasing the Bible into *The Message*. In his work on Matthew 5, Peterson described somewhat lengthy negotiations with the publishers, trying to convince them to use his preferred interpretation. As he studied the etymology of the repeated benediction, "Blessed are they . . . ," he felt the best word choice for the paraphrase would be "Lucky are they." It wasn't only his study that inspired this unusual suggestion, but his memory of one member of his congregation—an artist and well-read woman who was, nevertheless, new to hearing even the most well-known stories of the Bible. During a series when Peterson taught on the life of David, she approached him after the sermon to say, "I feel so lucky. I never heard that story before." Every Sunday after that, she said the same thing: "I feel so lucky. I never heard that story before."

Not surprisingly, Peterson's editors didn't take his suggestion and retained the familiar term "blessed." During the conference, the moderator asked Pastor Peterson, "When we read that portion in *The Message*, we could read that as 'lucky?'"

With an almost devilish grin, Eugene Peterson responded, "Yes. You could."

And ever since attending the symposium Brian and I read the Sermon on the Mount as the "Lucky-are-theys." Of course, *lucky* is a loaded word, and without the context of the rest of Jesus' teaching, we could easily misunderstand what his passage describes. Are we lucky when things fall apart because of some twisted, pietistic thinking that whatever doesn't kill us will make us stronger? No. Lucky because Christ has redeemed us to share in his blessing of belovedness and to share in his suffering for the hope of future glory; to share in the sufferings of this world as one of a broken people, longing for wholeness and redemption? Yes. Lucky to know the peace and to pass the peace of Christ around indiscriminately to our neighbors and family, and to our own fearful selves? Also, yes.

I'd like to suggest that *blessed* could also be described as a loaded word. For years, I read this passage as another checklist for things I needed to do to gain God's blessing. But the Beatitudes aren't a list of things to do, they are a list of things to be and, in fact, which we already are as members of God's beloved community. The "blessed are they's" name our true selves. Who am I? In Christ, I am poor in spirit, merciful, meek, hungering and thirsting for righteousness, making peace, and facing persecution. I am blessed.

My identity as a follower of Christ—baptized into his death, raised into his life, welcomed into full communion with the triune God and reconciled to give and receive that communion to all of God's image bearers—names me as already blessed. Already lucky. Jesus' sermon in Matthew 5 doesn't invite us to *do* as much as to live into our being as ones who share the cup of Jesus' suffering and the blessed spacious place of Jesus' resurrection.

Now—in contrast to the false narrative I lived for years, that my family was to be an extraordinary example of spiritual perfection—my Rule of Life grounds me in a different story, spacious enough for ordinary love that holds us together in our imperfections. After thirty-plus years of trying my very hardest and discovering that, on my best days, my very hardest still didn't make room for all that my family and I need, I now rest in the understanding that my children and husband were intended to have a perfect mom and wife and that I was intended to have perfect children and husband, and every one of us is out of luck. At the same time, held together in the extraordinary love of Jesus, who redeems our forced routines and imperfect love and who shares his father's blessing of belovedness, I know that we are the luckiest.

SIX BLESSINGS: A BENEDICTION FOR YOUR RULE

How can a Rule of Life remain intact in the paradoxes of God's kingdom, where the last are first and the end of the road is where we find blessing? What are the kingdom tensions held within a robust rule of life?

Six blessed tensions in a spacious Rule of Life

"Those who genuinely seek God change direction," writes author Trevor Hudson. "They turn and they keep turning until they turn right round."[4] He's describing something like the Benedictine vow of *conversatio*, or as we've described earlier in the book, a commitment to change. But I think this is also a meaningful description of our identity as blessed that Jesus defines in the Sermon on the Mount. As we seek God's direction, a Rule of Life is a spacious path to "keep turning until [we] turn right around." As I've practiced a Rule of Life in the context of Jesus' invitations in Matthew 5 to be as he is, blessed, I've considered six tensions that I can live into more fully. I offer them here for your reflection as a blessing on you and your rule.

May practices of celebration and lament make space for you to be blessed as one who mourns and one who is poor in spirit. May you know through humble, prayerful listening and loving, embodied presence that you are comforted and able to give comfort, and that you live in a kingdom that has no end.

May practices of work and rest make space for you to be blessed as one who is meek, content with who you are, beloved in God. May you know through humble, prayerful listening and loving, embodied presence that you will inherit the earth and that you already own everything that can't be bought.

May practices of worshiping God inside and outside the church walls make space for you to be blessed as pure in heart, present to God's presence in every place God chooses to arrive. May you know through humble, prayerful listening and loving, embodied presence that you will see God.

May practices of fasting and feasting make space for you to be blessed as one who hungers and thirsts for righteousness. May you know through humble, prayerful listening and loving, embodied presence that you will be filled.

May practices of giving and receiving hospitality make space for you to be blessed as one who is mercifully loving to your neighbors as you are to yourself. May you know through humble, prayerful listening and loving, embodied presence that you will receive mercy.

May practices of following Jesus into his death and resurrection make space for you to be blessed as one whose commitment to God provokes persecution. May you know through humble, prayerful listening and loving, embodied presence that yours is the kingdom of heaven.

BLESSING A RULE OF LIFE ON THE SPACIOUS PATH

He brought me out into a spacious place; he rescued me because he delighted in me.

—PSALM 18:19

This is my God, who is for me
who then is against me now?
He will breathe life into my words
and hold my feet to the ground.

—NATALIE MURPHY, "A PRAYER TO THE TRINITY"[1]

Read Matthew 5:1–12 slowly and, if possible, out loud a couple of times. What word or phrase catches your attention? How does your body feel as you read Jesus' words blessing the tensions of our lives with him? What questions come to mind? What do you need help with to say yes to Jesus' invitation? Could you put that need into a one-sentence prayer for help?

FOR FURTHER REFLECTION

1. How did the description of walking a labyrinth around the 180-degree turns resonate with you? Was it easier to imagine in terms of biblical repentance or in terms of biblical lament? How might this sentence inform your practice of a Rule of Life: "Sometimes the invitations of Jesus feel like heart-breaking tension before they feel like unforced rhythms of grace"?

2. At first glance and without analyzing your answers, which of the statements about spacious hospitality are you most drawn to? Which are you least drawn to?

3. Chapter 13, "Cruciform Love," invites us to consider how loving Jesus, others, and ourselves leads us to repentance. How have you experienced a connection between listening and repentance? Repentance and rest?

4. What is your experience with lament? How is your daily life formed by suffering?

5. What is your experience with resurrection joy? How is your daily life formed by celebration?

6. At first glance and without analyzing your answers, which of the kingdom tensions described in chapter 14 feel overwhelming to you right now? In which tension do you sense God's invitation to come to Jesus for rest right now?

7. As you continue to notice the everyday pattern of your life with gentle curiosity rather than reflexive judgment, what experiences or practices from this section feel most inviting to your Rule of Life? Share your response with a trusted friend. Ask them to simply pray for you.

FURTHER PRACTICES FOR CONTEMPLATION AND COMMUNITY: PRAYER OF DAILY EXAMEN AND CONTEMPLATIVE ACTIVISM

Welcoming God's calls to lament and repentance help me say yes to Jesus' invitation to spacious hospitality. Here are a couple of practices that have become essential to blessing my Rule of Life on a spacious path.

Prayer of Examen

The daily prayer of examen practices awareness of God's presence within the normal rhythms of your everyday life, and provides another historic Christian practice that helps us with the ongoing discernment for a Rule of Life. First modeled by St. Ignatius of Loyola, this prayer practice has remained a dynamic, deeply meaningful way to develop our capacity to hear God and our own hearts as well.

As you live in the tension of freedom and commitment within your Rule of Life, build in regular time for gentle assessment. Some people choose to pray an examen at the end of each day or the end of each week. I've found mornings are best for me as I think about the day before and look forward to the day ahead. You can spend as long as you'd like with this prayer—as few as five minutes can make a difference.

As you think back over a day or a week, notice the moments that felt the freest and most spacious. Notice the moments that felt constrictive and overly weighed down. Over time patterns will emerge that, with the guidance of the Holy Spirit through prayer, scripture, and community, help you understand better what daily work and practices Jesus is calling you to live and what ones he may be inviting you to release.

Daily examen

Start with silence. Take some time to be silent, without any noise or distraction, to pause and calmly think about the last few hours or days.

As you become aware of yourself—mind, body, and emotions—in God's presense, pray through the following questions:

1. *How can I look at my week/day with God's eyes, not merely my own?* In the company of Jesus, ask God to help you recall the movements and events of the past day or week.

2. *Where am I noticing gratitude?* Give thanks to God for each recollection that stirs a grateful heart.

3. *Which moments or events drew me inward to the center of my identity as a member of God's beloved community?* Where did I most easily recognize God's love that seeks and finds me? Savor the memory of intimacy with God, others, and yourself, giving thanks to Jesus for inviting you into God's belovedness.

4. *Which moments or events seemed to turn me away from the center of my identity as a member of God's beloved community? Where did I find it most difficult to recognize God's love that seeks and finds me?* Pay special attention to circumstances or tensions that might be indicators of God's kingdom at work. Ask the Holy Spirit to give voice to any lament you cannot express. Receive God's blessing. In addition, notice places you distanced yourself from God. Ask the Holy Spirit to help you confess, if needed. In the company of Jesus, acknowledge what you have done or left undone that made it difficult for you to connect with the love of God and others. Receive God's forgiveness.

5. *Where do I need Jesus to help me begin again?* In the company of Jesus, look forward to the day or week to come.

Ask the Holy Spirit to help you remain centered in your identity as one of God's beloved community. Ask for words to name the ways you need help seeking and finding God in any area of your life that feels fragmented or burdensome. Trust Jesus to shoulder the weight of your need for rest. Settle into that rest for a silent moment or two.

End your time with a simple prayer or chorus.

Go back into your day in Jesus' unforced rhythms of grace.

The Daily Examen for Living as an Antiracist Person[2] adapted those five prayer prompts and added reflection questions to help us discern more specifically areas of our lives where we could see God changing us and areas we needed God to change us more. For example, under the third prompt—"Review your day; ask God to search your heart and mind to see how embedded thought patterns of bias might have affected you today"—we found the reflection questions: *Have I done anything to diminish the image of God in my neighbor, friend, colleague, or family members that are persons of color? Did I say hurtful words to someone or about someone because of their race? Have I been silent when I could have spoken peace and truth into a racially biased or explicitly racist situation?* Under prompt number five—"Look toward tomorrow; think of how you might collaborate more effectively with God's heart to extend brotherly and sisterly love"—a few more questions for prayerful listening: *How can I speak up, show up and affirm people of color in my life? in society? What action can I take tomorrow to nourish the longing for racial justice? Are there things that need to be undone? Is there someone to whom I need to apologize? Is there someone to whom I need to reach out?*

CONTEMPLATIVE ACTIVISM

One of the most important decisions we make in contemplative silence is to discern God's presence in the real world around us. As we grow in discernment, we better understand how to respond to God's presence with prayerful action. We've already dispelled the myth that contemplation is about doing nothing and considered how prayerful listening to Spirit, scripture, creation, our lives, and silence leads us into prayerful acts of obedience.

African American spiritual leaders have led this conversation and embodied this flow from prayer into action. In her book *Soul Care in African American Practice*, author Dr. Barbara L. Peacock—quoting writer Dr. Ruth Haley Barton—offered the surprising observation that identifies Dr. Martin Luther King Jr. as one of the tremendous spiritual contemplatives of the twentieth century:

> Dr. Ruth Haley Barton, founder of the Transforming Center, affirmed the inclusion of contemplation and prayerfulness in his life when, in honor of Martin Luther King Day in January 2010, she wrote that Dr. King's "life was characterized by a powerful integration of prayer and contemplation with a profound commitment to decisive and loving action in the world." Barton's insight is extremely valuable in the discussion of the power of prayer and spiritual direction from an African American perspective.[3]

ORDINARY AND (EXTRAORDINARY) JUSTICE

On my eighteenth birthday, I visited my dad in jail. He was serving a light sentence for an act of nonviolent protest. As a pastor in our community, he believed he had a prophetic and pastoral responsibility to enact visible acts of peace and justice. His choice did not make him popular, and after the organization he participated in crumbled under leadership scandal and a shift toward inciting violence, I questioned my dad too. In the light of history, I've changed my mind. I wish more pastors and church leaders would be like my dad, who willingly sacrificed his reputation for a loving, embodied presence on behalf of the vulnerable.

One of the gifts of growing up in the church has been bearing witness to the hidden works of justice happening around me all the time when humble, loving people commit to listen prayerfully and then act on behalf of the poor, imprisoned, sick, homeless, orphaned, widowed, trafficked, abused, unemployed, and refugees among us. In our small congregation now, a small group of fiercely faithful women meets regularly to pray against the epidemic of sex trafficking in our city and the world. If you stumbled into the room without knowing why they were gathered, you'd have no idea that these nice church ladies' prayers bloom into fruitful acts of justice like painting rooms in homes for women who have survived sex trafficking, driving them to the store, listening to their stories, and offering a gentle, loving presence. Without this group of women, our church could move right along, unaware of the victims we encounter as we go about our city. Their embodied, prayerful presence serves as a stone in the wheels of our church. Because of this group of women, my friend Jennifer in particular, our church can't move forward without tending to the needs of the trafficked in our city.

We see this kind of action—from shouts for peace and justice to acts of hidden resistance—at work in the lives of religious communities since the time of the early church and across the ecumenical spectrum. Sharing the work of prayerful, embodied presence is how the Holy Spirit invites the church

to practice resurrection of God's kingdom come on earth as
it is in heaven. As we draw closer to God in contemplation
and community, we are more aware of how and where to join
God's action in the here and now.

BEGINNING AGAIN

[W]hat we now sense as a wide-open space is a graced experience of the real wide-open space, at whose center is the river of life, the tree of healing for the nations, and the throne of God, with whom we will dwell forever, face-to-face (Rev 22:1–5).

— SUSAN P. CURRIE[1]

Always we begin again.

— SAINT BENEDICT

Always, we begin again. I keep Benedict's famous four-word encouragement in a frame on my desk. Next to it I've placed two adorable but also kind of hilarious felted replicas of Brian and me made by my friend Jen. With unspooled colored felt and needles, she crafted me with my white hair and plump body, and Brian with his priest's stole and friendly face, dressed in the clothes we wore on one of our first Sundays with our new congregation in Connecticut. There the two little caricatures of us sit on the shelf, surrounded by photos of our children and Benedict's invitation: Always we begin again.

Our creator knows our tendencies to pendulum between unfettered freedom and over-structured commitments. The same God who, as G.K. Chesterton famously imagines, commands the sun to rise each day like a child at play who says "Do it again,"[2] invites us to begin again. We practice a Rule of Life on a spacious path when we live in this "quiet miracle of repetition."[3] Unfortunately, I don't always recognize the miraculous in repetition. Like Peter hatching plans to duplicate the glowing presence of a transfigured Jesus, I often miss that the actual miracle of repetition is the voice of Jesus inviting me to center again and again to rest in his belovedness with God. Once again, I needed to learn this truth scurrying around Ireland with a bucket list of my own plans for rest.

SEEKING AND BEING FOUND—AGAIN

During our sabbatical in the summer of 2022, we returned to several of the same locations in Ireland we had visited during our second honeymoon in 2016. We did not repay Father Donovan a visit, but we thought of him often and wished him well as we drove a wide berth around County Limerick. We knew we couldn't exactly replicate our first visit, but we treated a few of the places—a particular cliff walk winding around the southwest corner of Ireland, an ancient well of one of Ireland's first Christians, the shorefront seafood place that makes our favorite fish and chips—as a kind of pilgrimage. I'm embarrassed to admit that this little itinerary of return visits left us feeling more disappointed than refreshed the second time around. The day we went back to the cliff walk that took our breath away in 2016, we only worked up an irritating sweat in the unexpectedly blazing Irish sun. The well was fine but not quite as magical the second time around, and the fish and chip shop was closed the day we showed up—starving and overly eager for an exact recreation of our first visit.

We discovered, instead, our deepest experiences of rest during our sabbatical visit came in the places we didn't expect—the spontaneous stops along the side of the road to stand in the wind and rain and stare at the crash of the Atlantic Ocean carving into grassy cliffs, the just-in-the-nick-of-time encounter with neighborly locals who helped us find our way home from the middle of a sheep meadow where we'd been walking in circles, the hunt for a prayer labyrinth hidden behind a sturdy church building in a small Irish village. Once again I'd carried a checklist of spiritual experiences with me to a time intended for rest—a time we'd been given to just be and not to do. Once again, Jesus—without an ounce of irony or irritation—invited me to come to him for rest, to watch and pray with him so that I could discern the actual ways the Holy Spirit chose to reveal to us God's loving presence.

CIRCLING VICIOUS ROADS

In 2013, not long after I returned from the silent retreat where I had first encountered the restful rhythms of a prayer labyrinth, I found myself once again in the middle of Austin traffic, completely enraged. In an act of sheer fury, I flipped off a guy behind me at a stop sign. While my kids were in the car with me. And my daughter was in the driver's seat.

Yes. I did that. And I regret it to this day.

The truth is that, in the moment, it felt good to vent my unspent anger on someone—anyone. The man had driven behind us for a few blocks and repeatedly blasted his car horn at my daughter, a new driver trying to learn her way through the maze of central Austin. I'm not sure what was bothering him. Maybe she wasn't pushing through the intersections as quickly as he'd like, or maybe he just needed someone to be the scapegoat for his own road rage. Either way, he did more than blow his horn, he pushed my buttons. Big time.

At the intersection of weary frustration and mama-bear fight instincts, I thought that jerking my head, crooking my elbow, and letting the middle digit of my right hand stand tall was a way to protect my daughter. And it felt really, really good—for about fifteen seconds. Until I noticed the baby in the back seat of the other driver. This man I'd chosen to offer my sloppy violence was a parent too. My own daughter made it clear that she did not feel protected by my rage. Not even a little bit. Later that week—after I'd apologized to my family, especially to my daughter, and after I'd asked God to please forgive me and somehow make peace with this stranger with whom I'd never be able to make amends—my family was finally able to articulate what we'd been feeling every time we got in the car since we'd moved to Texas over two years prior: we felt disrespected. Austin's roadways and traffic rules were not designed with human beings' needs in mind. The streets were designed for the number of cars in an older, idealized version of Austin as a big city with a small-town persona. The result was that, by the time we arrived, uninitiated and inexperienced, city planners were trying to force hundreds of thousands of new vehicles into outdated street grids. We felt like critters in a city maze that exhausted us every single day.

Who ever thought infrastructure could compel such strong emotion? Lots of people, actually. Among those I'm most familiar with is the American novelist and environmental activist Wendell Berry, who's given his entire life provoking a spacious imagination to tend the world in unforced, natural rhythms. In *Art of the Commonplace*, a collection of essays that offer an agrarian alternative to the disintegrating forces of an industrially-optimized culture, Berry describes the inherent gift of a pathway as a "ritual of familiarity."[4] A path "through experience and familiarity, of movement to place; it obeys the natural contours; such obstacles as it meets it goes around." Roads, on the other hand, embody a "resistance against the landscape." Intended to hurry us along by avoiding the natural landscape, a road is "destructive, seeking to remove or destroy all obstacles in its way."

If we listen, we can hear this message from the indigenous peoples who crisscrossed the primitive landscapes, tamping down pathways that honored, befriended even, the natural contours of the earth.[5] Paths are forged by humans on a human scale, roads are forged by machines on an inhuman scale. Writer Margaret Feinberg notes that Wendell Berry's definition of paths evokes the narrow gate Jesus invites us to enter in Matthew 7:13–14—the narrow gate that "leads to life," in contrast to a "broad . . . road that leads to destruction." What's the difference then, Feinberg queries, between the broad road and narrow path? A narrow path is made for intimacy, inviting us to travel with a "sense of expectation and exploration, a need to pay attention and be mindful, a willingness to change direction and adapt."[6] Austin's roads, like most roads, were not made for exploration and made no space for us to readjust. In Austin, we were human beings trying to flourish in a system that prioritized machines at all costs. We needed space to acclimate without putting our lives in danger; we needed room for us to be human beings trying to make our way from one place to the next.[7]

When Jesus invites us to come to him for rest, he is inviting us, not despite our human tendencies to force our lives into ill-fitting systems, but because of them. His invitation embraces our humanity and invites us to live in rhythms best suited for us because they are designed by the creator of humanity. Machines require manufactured repetition designed for continuous, cookie-cutter outcomes. Human beings need rhythms of both freedom and structure, which means the results may vary. To be human is to be able to receive the grace to begin again. To be a Christian is to be able to receive the grace to begin again in the company of Jesus. What's the difference, then, between a broad road and a spacious path? The spacious path leads us always and ever into the mystery of God's belovedness. The broad road is built for efficiency of outcomes, the spacious path is created for intimacy. As we walk, we become more like Jesus and more like the true self God has always imagined us to be.

That day when I let road rage mar the shape of God's loving presence in me, I was frustrated, yes, and humbled. I had only just begun to make peace with the tensions of living in an unfamiliar city in a new season of life. I'd have preferred to remain as peaceful as I felt walking that labyrinth at the retreat center and yet, there I was, back where I'd started from—sad, mad, and behaving badly in front of my family and neighbors. The lesson of the labyrinth, though, is that even when we're back where we started—at the entrance to the path—we are not at a dead end; we remain on the same path that always leads us home. Practicing a Rule of Life, like walking a path, makes room for adaptation, and echoes the lesson of the labyrinth: the Rule as a spacious path will always reorient us to the center as we begin again.

THREE VIRTUES: A RULE FOR HOLDING TOGETHER A VIRTUOUS—NOT VICIOUS—CIRCLE

How do I know if what I'm discerning for a Rule of Life is a spacious path? What practices will help me remain in Jesus' unforced rhythms of grace?

Balance, Harmony, Moderation

The labyrinth is a visual symbol of balance and harmony, serving the human affinity for aesthetic symmetry and kinesthetic equilibrium with mathematical precision. These values are also embedded in the spiritual practice of a Rule of Life. Nothing, in my opinion, is more essential to the staying power of Benedict's rule than these three values: balance, harmony, and moderation.

During our sabbatical we worshiped one Sunday morning in London's Westminster Cathedral. Reverend Robert Latham, in his reflection on that Sunday's lectionary passages, which included Hebrews 11's description of the substance of faith, invited us to surrender the habits of a "vicious circle" so that we can step into the virtuous circle where Jesus lives.[8] When Father Bob (he told me I could call him that after the service) spoke about the virtuous circle, he was speaking of faith, hope, and love, but I couldn't help but hear the Benedictine virtues of balance, harmony, and moderation. These three values shape a Rule of Life that helps us move away from the vicious circles of our striving for productivity and significance into a virtuous and spacious path that leads us again and again into the center of God's belovedness. Balance, moderation, and harmony set the pace for Jesus' unforced rhythms of grace.

As virtues, balance, harmony, and moderation become part of the way we navigate the world, but they also help us shape the framework for a Rule of Life. Here are some ways the three virtues can help you as you discern the content of your Rule.

BALANCE LEVELS OF DIFFICULTY

"Uphill" and "downhill" practices[9]

I'm adapting John Mark Comer's terms of "upstream" and "downstream" practices to remain with our metaphor of walking a Rule of Life as a spacious path. No matter which imagery you feel most drawn to, both rowing a boat and hiking a hill work to describe the tensions we hold within a robust Rule of Life. Uphill practices include things that—because of our season of life, natural temperament, or other constraints—are more difficult for us. Downhill practices are things that come more naturally. Think of the challenge of hiking uphill as opposed to the relative ease of walking downhill. Generally, a balanced Rule of Life includes a few uphill practices and a lot of downhill practices to make room for rest, even while the Holy Spirit expands our capacity and helps us to become more like Jesus and more like our true selves.

Analog and digital habits

A spacious twenty-first-century Rule of Life balances analog (physical, in-person, tangible) and digital (virtual, intangible, remote) habits. Depending on your personality, you probably gravitate to one side of this spectrum or the other. I'd guess that most of us, like much of our culture, need to intentionally include more tactile, hands-on, human-paced activities in our lives, but that's not always the case. All of us—even monks!—need to cultivate both analog and digital habits to offer prayerful listening and loving presence to the world. We need practices that engage our minds as well as our hands to help us embrace rhythms of spacious work and Sabbath rest.

EMBRACE MODERATION IN EVERYTHING

In *Wisdom Distilled from the Daily*, Sister Joan Chittister writes that in Benedict's Rule, "All must be given its due, but only its due. There should be something of everything and not too much of anything."[10] We hear the apostle Paul's description in Romans 12:1–2 of an ordinary life of worship in Benedict's rule that all things—eating, drinking, sleeping, reading, working, and praying—should be done in moderation.

Discern what is doable

Earlier in the book, I shared Joan Chittister's reassuring reminder that Benedict's rule distinguishes itself from the "swings toward spiritual extremism and perfectionism" that have characterized the church for centuries by offering "normalcy as the will of God." In the sister's words, a Benedictine Rule of Life "asks only what is doable."[11] Within a Rule, we're making space to discern what is doable at any given time in our lives and to adjust when needed—which for many of us will be frequently. As a spacious path, a Rule of Life is a spiritual practice that develops our capacity to be flexible—to hold together both stability and change.

Embrace a middle way

Throughout each chapter of the book, I've invited us to imagine rules for holding together parts of the world and our lives that feel like irresolvable tensions. For example, the invitations of Jesus in Matthew 11:28–30 offer a rule for holding together work and rest. Jesus' words to the law expert in Luke 10 offer us a rule for holding together law and love as well as love for God, neighbors, and ourselves. In Romans 12:1–2, we hear a rule that holds together parts of our lives we might consider "secular" with the parts we might call "spiritual," when worshiping God with our whole heart, soul, mind, and strength means that everything we do is a spiritual discipline. The Anglican tradition of *via media* or "middle way" speaks well to this virtue of moderation. While this term is often misunderstood to mean indecision or passivity—walking the middle of the road instead of aligning with one side or another—instead it's an intentional discipline to hold the virtue of moderation in all things. As Charles Simeon, rector of Holy Trinity Church in Cambridge, England, once said, "The truth is not in the middle, and not in one extreme; but in both extremes." In theological practice, *via media* allows us to integrate the most essential truths on both sides of a question or issue into one perspective. A Rule of Life provides structure for approaching our lives from this middle way and makes space to hold together in creative tension the parts of life that seem opposed.

If/then decision making

"If/then" decision-making is another best practice that helps me keep the commitments of my Rule of Life in the freedom of moderation. It works like this: If A happens, then I respond with backup plan B. For example, if the weekend schedule gets overbooked, then I clear everything from Monday. If I don't take a walk in the morning, then at 4:00 p.m. I walk no matter what else is happening at that time. If I don't see my mom in any given month, then I call her on a specific day to catch up. If Brian has to work on his regularly scheduled day off, then he picks another day next week to take off instead. Hopefully, you get the idea. If/then decision making frees me from feeling I need to make constant decisions in order to practice my Rule of Life and makes space to order my days within abundant rhythms of grace.

Live in the seasons

Allow the seasons of the calendar (church and civic) to serve you as rhythms of grace to express the full range of Christian worship, including practices of work and rest, gathered worship and outside mission, loving your neighbor and yourself, fasting and feasting, giving and receiving, lament and celebration, silence and joyful noise, and more. The liturgical seasons help us navigate all the ways we long to worship God into one spacious path, much like the four seasons of my hometown helped me navigate my daily travel. An example: Rather than following the whims of my appetite or society's standards for eating, I lean toward a simple diet with some fasting in the seasons of Lent and Advent and feasting at Christmastide and Eastertide. This doesn't mean I never have to consider what I eat and drink any other time, but the liturgical seasons of feasting and fasting serve to establish what moderation looks like the rest of the year.

SEEK HARMONY

Where balance and moderation serve to hold together difference or tensions, harmony seeks to emphasize the similarities of a tension into one cohesive whole. In musical terms, harmony is the result of many notes coming together into a pleasing chord. We hear the individual notes but as one whole sound. Harmony is what we mean when we describe the unity in diversity in God's beloved community as beautiful. It's the new thing that emerges from separate things coming together as a whole. In many ways, harmony is more a *fruit* of our Rule than the *practices* that make up the Rule. Seeking harmony is a vital practice for discernment as we practice a Rule of Life.

Ask "What's missing?"

In balance, we're learning to toggle between two different kinds of things. In moderation, we're learning to pare down different things to their most essential expression. And in harmony, we're learning to create one new expression out of many different things. A soloist singing a cappella can embrace moderation and balance in the volume, rhythm, and vocal range of her performance but she can't embrace harmony. She needs another voice or instrument to do that. As we're discerning a Rule of Life, sometimes we need to seek harmony by asking "Who or what is missing?" For example, I recognized that I needed to actively, intentionally build stories and relationships and prayer practices with people of color into my Rule of Life. Without their voices, my rule lacks harmony.

Learn from disharmony

Invite tender awareness to the parts of your Rule that feel disharmonious or "out of tune" as you continue to welcome discernment through practices of prayerful, humble listening, and loving, embodied presence. When we hear a noise that is grating, our tendency is to find a way to avoid that noise or a way to remove it altogether. Blocking noise is fine for trying to have a conversation on your phone in the middle of a crowded coffee shop, but for walking a Rule of Life on a spacious path, we need to be able to discern and learn from the parts of our lives—the jobs, relationships, practices, and habits—that create disharmony. Sometimes the end result is to take something away (like the Spanx I used to wear to pretend I was a different shape but that caused me incessant and significant discomfort) but sometimes disharmony is an indicator that something needs to be added. *Lectio divina* is a perfect example of how seeking harmony helped me discern a Rule of Life. For most of my life, I flourished from a regular practice of inductive Bible study and theological teaching. At the point in my life that I was walking through intensive counseling and therapy for my childhood trauma, I found that I couldn't read the Bible in the same way. It felt heavy and mechanical. I longed for the life of scripture but needed a new way to live in scripture. Now I'm able to balance both of those practices in my Rule of Life, but I wouldn't have arrived at balance had I not had help discerning the disharmony.

FIVE BEST PRACTICES: A RULE FOR BEGINNING AND BEGINNING AGAIN ON THE SPACIOUS PATH

1. Begin and begin again with a rule for rest and prayer.

Start by setting aside one day a week to rest and worship God. We talked more in depth about the practice of Sabbath earlier in the book. If you don't yet enjoy a regular day of Sabbath, begin there. That, for now, is your Rule of Life.

Next, consider how rest and prayer form the ordinary days of your life. In particular, pay attention to the transition parts of your day—nighttime to morning, morning to midday, midday to evening, and evening to nighttime. Consider also how rest and prayer help you respond to interruptions and unexpected changes to your plans for the day. Each of the moments can serve like a church bell calling you to prayer and to a moment of Sabbath rest.

No matter what else you include, build your rule around daily prayer and weekly Sabbath rest. Start where you are and not where you think you should be. Let Jesus' invitation to come to him for rest be your guide.

2. Be specific.

In the healing prayer ministry in which I serve, we use the guideline "Be specific, not vague and not detailed." This is not only for the sake of efficiency, as a way to save time in order to fit in more prayer. We find this helpful also because there's power in naming things. When I can say "Make eye contact with my kids each day" rather than "Be a good parent," I'm naming a doable practice that helps me notice my love for my kids and what may be making it difficult to express that love. When I can say "Cease work from 6:00 a.m. to 6:00 p.m. on Sunday" instead of "Keep the Sabbath," I'm naming an act of worship rather than an ideal. This is how we discern the difference between embracing the reality of our lives and perpetuating an idealized version of our lives. Being specific is not a way to pursue perfection, but discernment. Being specific rather than abstract energizes a Rule of Life into a living, breathing practice.

3. Find an inviting format.

As we continue to notice without judgment our "default" settings throughout our days and as we continue to listen to Jesus' invitations and commands in the company of the Holy Spirit and trusted friends, what format best helps us gather our responses to those invitations into a memorable and meaningful document? The best answer to this question is to feel free to find the method most helpful to you. Begin this step by making the question part of your discernment process: What is the most life-giving format for me to record a Rule of Life right now?

You could keep a journal, draw a poster, create a spreadsheet, or make a list. (Yes, after all my list-making angst when I was first learning to practice a Rule of Life, I actually keep mine in a series of lists.) Many people find artistic expression—rather than written words—meaningful.[12] I've seen people record their Rule of Life drawn as color and imagery on a canvas, sketched in a journal, captured as a collage of photographs, and written in poetic verse. My friend Karen drew her Rule of Life in the shape of a labyrinth with key words from her Rule written within the circular lines. Her Rule of Life gave me the framework for this entire book.

In your rough drafts, use whatever method works best for you. Start by reflecting on your experience with the practices at the end of each section of the book. While I think it would be most helpful to work your way through the book chronologically, you could jump in wherever you feel most drawn. As you do, keep noticing your daily habits and practices without judgment.

Let yourself reflect in a spacious way—in conversations with friends, family, Bible study groups, or a spiritual director, and while you're listening to God in silence, scripture, and prayer. Pay attention to what you feel about practicing a Rule in your body, thoughts, and feelings. Reflect while you're walking the dog, running on a treadmill, or stretching your aching muscles at the end of the day. Make space to reflect while you do creative projects—holding your questions and responses lightly while you draw, cook a meal, make a craft with your kids, or read a novel. Notice what it feels like to think about practicing a Rule of Life in your everyday, mundane habits—taking a shower, paying your bills, brushing your teeth, making small talk with the neighbor, washing the dishes, or putting gas in the car. Bring your questions and responses with you into your work tasks—answering emails, bagging groceries, sitting through meetings, changing diapers, or grading papers. One of the most fruitful ways to discern a Rule of Life is to do it while you're living the day-in and day-out of your actual life. Keep paying attention to the desires that sometimes hide beneath your daily habits. Know that all these things themselves are acts of worship to our Creator who loves us so well.

4. Sum it up simply.

Naturally, as I've been writing this book, I've been thinking a lot about how I discern, record, and practice my own Rule of Life and if I could say, like Jesus, "Learn from me; watch how I do it." In full disclosure, and maybe to no surprise as someone who's just written sixty thousand words about it, my Rule of Life is wordy and not something I could share as template for you to replicate. Knowing how helpful it is to learn from someone else's practical example, I've wondered how I could simplify the words into something that's easier to communicate.

As I pondered this, I thought again about Jesus' words to the law expert in Luke 10. Essentially, every word Jesus ever spoke and every choice he made provide us with the perfect Rule of Life. But, when asked to sum up the entire message of the Law and the Prophets, he gave us two commandments:

Love the Lord with all your heart, soul, and mind.
Love your neighbor as yourself.

I have also been reading the Rules of the church's saints. Benedict and Francis seem to get the most press, but I keep coming back to Dorothy Day's Rule of Life:

See the face of Christ in the poor.
And: journal every day.[13]

I'm struck by the dailiness of her Rule: moment by moment, see the face of Christ in the poor and keep a daily journal. Obviously, her life was full of complexity, creating and recreating communities to care for the poor. But at the end of the day, she summed up her Rule in this simple way.

I have decided that the simple words that best capture the Rule of Life I believe I'm called to live are words I've shared countless times—three simple directives that sum up the way I hope to daily respond to Jesus' invitations that orient my life to the center of God's belovedness:

Worship God.

Love people.

Enjoy beauty.

Perhaps you hear the echo of the greatest commandments there? This is not the whole of my Rule of Life—it's not specific enough and doesn't help me remember the practices that help me live these three invitations. Over time, living with the practice through different seasons and in the company of friends helping me to discern, these three statements emerged from my Rule of Life, rather than dictated it to me. It's a gift that keeps on giving, because I can now take those three statements with me when I need to make adjustments to my Rule. It's kind of like a title of a song—enough to help me recall the lyrics and the melody, but not the same thing as singing it out from the top of my lungs.

5. Make returning to your Rule Life, part of your Rule of Life.

While contemplation and community are daily practices that help us discern our Rule and adjust as we go, I find it helpful every once in a while to revisit my Rule of Life in a more formal way. As you look at the patterns of your life, you'll likely recognize certain times of year feel like natural "refresh" buttons. For many people, the beginning of fall, when a new school year begins, or the beginning of January, when a new calendar year begins, work well. Or, if you follow the rhythms of the liturgical year, you might make revisiting your Rule of Life part of your Advent or Lenten disciplines. One of my new rhythms in this season of life is to take an annual prayer and planning retreat with Brian early in September. We spend our days in individual prayer over our upcoming commitments and for our hopes and needs for the year. And then we pray and talk together at different times of the day. You might also find a ministry or church that offers Rule of Life retreats and use that time and space to reflect on your practices. Whatever you choose, let this be a time to listen to Jesus' invitations to return to the center of God's belovedness. Everything else orients to that incredible reality.

MAKE YOUR HOME IN MY LOVE

In John 15:1–17, Jesus gives his disciples the landmarks for their new normal: Abide in my love. This is how I love you. Love one another as I have loved you. You are my friends when you do this.[14] Jesus makes this simple announcement to the disciples, "I have named you friends because I've let you in on everything I've heard from the Father" (John 15:14–15, *The Message*). And we hear the echoes of his invitation to the law expert in Luke 10: *All the commandments and invitations of God boil down to this—love me and love one another. Remain in my love.* We also hear the spirit of invitation in Matthew 11: *Come to me; keep company with me. You are my friends. Make your home in my love.* In the loving companionship of Jesus, others, and our own souls we walk a Rule of Life as a spacious path that unfolds in front of us each day like a new mercy while always pointing us home into the center of God's love. Along the way, we listen for the direction of the Holy Spirit, who is always making everything new.

We begin again and again until all of our beginnings have led us to our eternal home. My friend and colleague Dr. Sue Currie says that as we become more aware of the spacious invitations of God "what we sense as a wide-open space is a graced experience of the real wide-open space, at whose center is the river of life, the tree of healing for the nations, and the throne of God, with whom we will dwell forever, face-to-face (Rev 22:1–5)."[15] The spacious path of a Rule of Life is this kind of "graced experience" that holds all the fragments of our lives together in the restful way of Jesus. The way of Jesus that leads us to our forever home. The place where, after all our seeking, we will be completely found, seeing Jesus, each other, and our own souls completely. Beloved, we will be home.

ACKNOWLEDGMENTS

This book found a spacious path because of the generosity of Michelle Van Loon and Marlena Graves, writing mentors who shared their savvy and resources, and the hospitality of Laura Leonard, an editor who welcomed my great outpouring of words and then, along with Elisabeth Ivey, helped me turn those words into a more welcoming format for others. Thank you to the steadfast theologian, writer, and friend W. David O. Taylor for being on-call through this entire project and to the editors who have welcomed me along the way and helped me shape words, some of which I've shared again in this book—Andi Ashworth, Andrea Bailey Willits, Chris Smith, Josh Larsen, Kari West, Ned Bustard, and Maureen Swinger. To the writers who've told stories on my website since 2006, thank you for keeping company with me. Thank you, especially, to Brendah Ndagire and Vernée Wilkinson for permitting me to share a few of your remarkable words in this book.

I'm thankful for the hospitality of the pastor's wives—Christine Warner who first invited me into restful silence, Sally Breedlove who first invited me to the life of a spiritual director, and Karen Stiller for inviting me to cherish the lament and the resurrection life of the minister's family. Thank you, especially to my first pastor's wife, Nancy Hill, for inviting me to love scripture and stories. I love you, Mom.

I've hoped to share the good welcome we've received in our church communities through the years—Union Center Christian Church in New York, Christ Church, and Church of the Cross in Austin, and now, our beloved Church of the Apostles in Bridgeport, Connecticut. Thank you to my first pastor, Douglas Hill, for inviting me to love the church. I love you, Dad.

Thank you, to Sue Currie and LTI for your spacious welcome into the Selah Rule of Life. To Elizabeth Fitch, my spiritual director, thank you for your prayerful listening and loving presence. Thank you to each person who has welcomed me as a spiritual director. You are beloved. Thank you especially to Karen Hutton, whose joyful practice of a Rule of Life helped me imagine the symbol of a prayer labyrinth in the first place.

In terms of spacious hospitality, thank you to Lois and Bill Barker for literally moving out of their cozy home for a few days so that I could write and reflect in a quiet space. And to Gillian Gilbourne, the most hospitable librarian in all of Ireland, thank you for sharing Millstreet Library with us when we needed a place to work during a season of rest. We've got our library cards and we will be back.

Thank you to Alicia Nichols, Amy and David McLaughlin, Amy Willers, Kaley Ehret, Karen Hutton, Kendra Jackson, Krista Vossler, Natalie Murphy, Phaedra Taylor, Shannon Coelho, and Walter Wittwer for welcoming various drafts of this manuscript into your full lives and for the compassion and skill of your insights. Thank you also to the band of family, friends, and church community who continually welcomed my need for prayer and shared the joy of this gift with me. Thank you especially to my delightful photographer friend

June Williams, who helped me enjoy an afternoon of posing for author headshots even though my knees were skinned, and my heart was breaking.

To MALT: thank you for teaching me friendship.

To the SQUAD: thank you for being ready to raise a glass with me at any time. I think I'm finally done now. To the Book Proposal and Sisters Voxer threads: thank you for being lightness and brightness, truth and grace, and beloved.

To Andrew, Alexander, Rebekah, Natalie, Jordan, Kendra, and Julian, thank you for your fierce and tender commitment to holding hands in times of trouble. You have made me the luckiest. To Brian, for being an essential part in everything I've ever given birth to and for being my first reader for every single word of this book. I very fancy you.

NOTES

INTRODUCTION

1. Guy Davenport, and Norman Wirzba, *The Art of the Commonplace: The Agrarian Essays of Wendell Berry* (New York: Counterpoint, 2003), 18.
2. Craig M. Wright, *The Maze and the Warrior: Symbols in Architecture, Theology, and Music* (Cambridge: Harvard University Press, 2001), 44, quoted in "Labyrinth of Chartres: Medieval Studies," Loyola University Chicago, accessed 2023, https://www.luc.edu/medieval/labyrinths/chartres.shtml.
3. "Saint Benedict," OSB DOT ORG, February 5, 2020, https://www.osb.org/our-roots/saint-benedict/.
4. "Saint Benedict," OSB DOT ORG.
5. "Saint Benedict," OSB DOT ORG.
6. "Rule of Saint Benedict," Wikimedia Foundation, February 7, 2023, https://en.wikipedia.org/wiki/Rule_of_Saint_Benedict.
7. Richard J. Foster, *Celebration of Discipline: The Path to Spiritual Growth* (San Francisco: HarperCollins, 1988), 7.
8. "The Holy Eucharist: Renewed Ancient Text," Anglican Church of North America, *The Book of Common Prayer and Administration of the Sacraments with Other Rites and Ceremonies of the Church According to the Use of the Anglican Church in North America: Together with the New Coverdale Psalter* (Huntington Beach, CA: Anglican Liturgy Press, 2019), 140.
9. "Regula (Architecture)," November 17, 2006, https://second.wiki/wiki/regula_architektur.
10. I'm indebted to my colleague and friend Vernée Wilkinson for this profound insight.
11. Joan Chittister, *Wisdom Distilled from the Daily: Living the Rule of St. Benedict Today* (New York: HarperCollins, 2013), 3–4.
12. Esther de Waal, *Seeking God: The Way of St. Benedict* (Collegeville, MN: Liturgical Press, 1984), 18–19.
13. John Gramlich, "Two Years into the Pandemic, Americans Inch Closer to a New Normal," March 3, 2022, Pew Research Center, https://www.pewresearch.org/2022/03/03/Two-Years-into-the-Pandemic-Americans-Inch-Closer-to-a-New-Normal/.

14. Susan Porterfield Currie, "Welcome to Selah," *Selah-East 2017 Orientation*. Reading presented at the Selah-East 2017 Orientation, 2015. Victoria Emily Jones, "A Spacious Place (Artful Devotion)," *Art & Theology*, October 8, 2019, https://artandtheology .org/2019/10/08/a-spacious-place-artful-devotion/.

15. Esther de Waal, *Seeking God*, 18.

PROLOGUE

1. John Stott, *Basic Christianity, Fiftieth Anniversary Edition* (Grand Rapids, MI: Eerdmans Publishing Company, 2012), 17.

2. Beatrice of Nazareth, *The Life of Beatrice of Nazareth*, trans. Roger De Ganck (Collegeville, MN: Cistercian Publications, 1991), pp. 289–331. Thanks to Plough for introducing me to this little-known medieval nun. "What Two Medieval Nuns Can Teach Us about Love," Plough, accessed February 9, 2023, https://www.plough .com/en/topics/faith/devotional-reading/what-two-medieval-nuns-can-teach-us-about-love?utm_source=Plough%2B-%2BEnglish&utm_campaign=ac1e647fab-Dig&utm_medium=email&utm_term=0_4cbb94afa4-ac1e647fab-295741949.

3. It seems I'm not alone in my experience of getting scolded by a monk. Rich Villodas, *The Deeply Formed Life: Five Transformative Values to Root Us in the Way of Jesus* (New York: Crown Publishing Group, 2020), 20.

4. Kathleen Norris, *Dakota: A Spiritual Geography* (Boston: Houghton Mifflin, 2001), 191.

5. T. S. Eliot. *Little Gidding* (London: Faber and Faber, 1944).

6. I'm thankful to Art House America for publishing a version of this story in 2017. Tamara Hill Murphy, "You Are Here to Kneel," Art House America, September 18, 2017, https://www.arthouseamerica.com/blog/you-are-here-to-kneel.html.

7. "Recognizing the Stranger: The Art of Emmanuel Garibay," Image Journal, October 29, 2020, https://imagejournal.org/article/recognizing-the-stranger/.

8. Dorothy Day, *The Reckless Way of Love: Notes on Following Jesus* (Walden, NY: Plough Publishing House, 2017).

9. Perhaps the best place to understand my friend and former pastor's wife Christine Warner's heart for the poor and marginalized is in the work she leads within the Anglican Church of North America, https://www.anglicanjusticeandmercy.org/ leadership-team.

10. Brendah Ndagire, "Practice Resurrection with Brendah Ndagire (Uganda)," *Tamara Hill Murphy*, March 31, 2021, https://www.tamarahillmurphy.com/ blogthissacramentallife/practice-resurrection-with-brendah-ndagire/2019/5/21.

11. When Jesus met the widow of Nain in Luke 7:13, the NRSVue uses "moved with compassion," which can also be translated as "his heart went out to her" (NIV) and "his heart broke" (*The Message*).

12. Brendah Ndagire, "Practice Resurrection."

13. David Vryhof, "Discernment in Prayer," *Selah Certificate Program in Spiritual Direction*, lecture, 2019.

14. Thomas Merton, *No Man is an Island* (Boulder, CO: Shambhala, 2005), 244.

PART 1

1. Esther de Waal, *Seeking God: The Way of St. Benedict* (Collegeville, MN: Liturgical Press, 1984), 97.

2. I'm thankful to Steve Macchia for this essential insight into Benedict's life of listening. Stephen A. Macchia, *Crafting a Rule of Life: An Invitation to the Well-Ordered Way* (London: InterVarsity Press, 2012), 15.

CHAPTER 1

1. Martha Graham "An Athlete of God," in *This I Believe: The Personal Philosophies of Remarkable Men and Women*, Dan Gediman, Jay Allison, John Gregory, Viki Merrick, eds. (New York: Henry Holt and Company, 2006), 84.
2. No one else is to blame for this paraphrase; it is entirely my own.
3. Esther de Waal, *Seeking God: The Way of St. Benedict* (Collegeville, MN: Liturgical Press, 1984), 39.

CHAPTER 2

1. Eugene Peterson, *Eat This Book* (London: Hodder & Stoughton, 2011).
2. Esther de Waal, *Seeking God: The Way of St. Benedict* (Collegeville, MN: Liturgical Press, 1984), 44.
3. *The Rule of St. Benedict in English* (Collegeville, MN: Liturgical Press, 2016), Prol. 49, quoted in de Waal, *Seeking God*, 44.
4. De Waal, *Seeking God,* 50.
5. De Waal, 50.
6. Dane C. Ortlund, *Gentle and Lowly: The Heart of Christ for Sinners and Sufferers* (Wheaton, IL: Crossway, 2020), 23.

CHAPTER 3

1. Steve Macchia, host, Tom Griffith, guest, "Discerning Our Personal Rule of Life," January 29, 2021, in *The Discerning Leader,* https://www.leadershiptransformations .org/podcast/2021/01/29/introduction-discerning-our-personal-rule-of-life-episode-01/.
2. Curt Thompson, *The Soul of Shame: Retelling the Stories We Believe About Ourselves* (Westmont, IL: InterVarsity Press, 2015), 138, quoted in Irwyn L. Ince, *The Beautiful Community: Unity, Diversity, and the Church at Its Best* (Westmont, IL: InterVarsity Press, 2020), 48.
3. Dorothy Day, *The Reckless Way of Love: Notes on Following Jesus* (Walden, NY: Plough Publishing House, 2017).

CHAPTER 4

1. Mary Oliver, *Upstream: Selected Essays* (New York: Penguin Publishing Group, 2019), 91.
2. Marilyn McEntyre, *Caring for Words in a Culture of Lies*, 2nd ed. (Grand Rapids, MI: Eerdmans, 2021).
3. Thomas Merton, *New Seeds of Contemplation* (Boston: Shambhala, 2003), 276.
4. J. R. R. Tolkien, *The Lord of the Rings* (United Kingdom: Houghton Mifflin, 2004), 105.
5. Steve Macchia, host, Tom Griffith, guest, "Discerning Our Personal Rule of Life Episode 01," January 29, 2021, in *The Discerning Leader,* 10:59, https://www .leadershiptransformations.org/podcast/2021/01/29/introduction-discerning-our-personal-rule-of-life-episode-01/.

6. "Rule of Life | Berkeley Divinity School," Berkeley Divinity School: the Episcopal Seminary at Yale, accessed February 14, 2023, https://berkeleydivinity.yale.edu/spiritual-formation/rule-life.

7. "Committed to Selah Shared Rule of Life," Leadership Transformations, accessed February 14, 2023, https://www.leadershiptransformations.org/directory-of-spiritual-directors/wpbdp_category/shared-rule-of-life/.

8. Jeannette A. Bakke, *Holy Invitations: Exploring Spiritual Direction* (Ada, MI: Baker Publishing Group, 2000), 36.

CHAPTER 5

1. Karen Stiller, *The Minister's Wife: A Memoir of Faith, Doubt, Friendship, Loneliness, Forgiveness, and More* (Carol Stream, IL: Tyndale House Publishers, 2020), 14.

2. Joan Chittister, quoted in Esther de Waal, *Seeking God: The Way of St. Benedict* (Collegeville, MN: Liturgical Press, 1984), 76–77.

CHAPTER 6

1. Malcolm Guite, "The Baptism of Christ," in *Sounding the Seasons: Seventy Sonnets for the Christian Year* (Norwich, UK: Canterbury Press, 2013), 20.

2. Esther De Waal, *Seeking Life: The Baptismal Invitation of the Rule of St. Benedict* (Collegeville, MN: Liturgical Press, 2017), 99.

3. Irwyn L. Ince, *The Beautiful Community: Unity, Diversity, and the Church at Its Best* (Westmont, IL: InterVarsity Press, 2020), 38.

4. Ince, *The Beautiful Community*, 35–36.

5. Ince, *The Beautiful Community*, 39.

6. Ince, *The Beautiful Community*, 41.

CHAPTER 7

1. William Butler Yeats, "The Second Coming," Poetry Foundation, n.d. , accessed February 16, 2023, https://www.poetryfoundation.org/poems/43290/the-second-coming.

2. Kate Bowler, *Everything Happens for a Reason: And Other Lies I've Loved* (New York: Random House Publishing Group, 2018), 80.

3. Fernando Ortega, "Children of the Living God," https://genius.com/Fernando-ortega-children-of-the-living-god-lyrics.

4. Brett Alan Dewing, "Come, Union." In *Take, Eat, Remember, and Believe* (CreateSpace Independent Publishing Platform, 2017), 82–83.

5. I'm grateful for the work of rabbi and family therapist Edwin H. Friedman for introducing Brian and me to this idea of non-anxious presence within a congregation, a theme found particularly in Section 3, "Congregation as a Family System," Edwin H. Friedman, *Generation to Generation: Family Process in Church and Synagogue* (New York: Guilford Publications, 2011).

RESPONSE TO PART 2

1. "Support Groups," NAMI, accessed February 20, 2023, https://nami.org/Support-Education/Support-Groups.

PART 3

1. Margaret Guenther, *At Home in the World: A Rule of Life for the Rest of Us* (New York: Church Publishing Incorporated, 2006), 13.
2. Cory Turner, "School Principals Say Culture Wars Made Last Year 'Rough as Hell,'" NPR, December 1, 2022, https://www.npr.org/2022/12/01/1139685828/schools-democracy-misinformation-purple-state.
3. Kim Parker and Juliana Menasce Horowitz, "Majority of Workers Who Quit a Job in 2021 Cite Low Pay, No Opportunities for Advancement, Feeling Disrespected," Pew Research Center, March 10, 2022, https://www.pewresearch.org/fact-tank/2022/03/09/majority-of-workers-who-quit-a-job-in-2021-cite-low-pay-no-opportunities-for-advancement-feeling-disrespected/.
4. Eli Rosenberg, "4.3 Million Americans Left Their Jobs in December as Omicron Variant Disrupted Everything," Washington Post, February 1, 2022, https://www.washingtonpost.com/business/2022/02/01/job-quits-resignations-december-2021/.
5. James Dean, "Pillemer: Family Estrangement a Problem 'Hiding in Plain Sight'," Cornell Chronicle, September 10, 2020. https://news.cornell.edu/stories/2020/09/pillemer-family-estrangement-problem-hiding-plain-sight.
6. David Brooks, "What's Ripping American Families Apart?" New York Times, July 29, 2021, https://www.nytimes.com/2021/07/29/opinion/estranged-american-families.html.
7. Margaret Guenther, *At Home in the World: A Rule of Life for the Rest of Us* (New York: Church Publishing Incorporated, 2006), 13.
8. Joan Chittister, *In God's Holy Light: Wisdom from the Desert Monastics* (Cincinnati, OH: Franciscan Media, 2013), 132–135, quoted in "Living the Interruptions: Exploring a Rule of Life for 2021," *Conversatio Divina*, January 22, 2022, https://conversatio.org/living-the-interruptions-exploring-a-rule-of-life-for-2021/.
9. Bishop Todd Hunter, "Reality Is Always Our Friend," *The Gospel of the Kingdom*, December 28, 2022, https://bishoptoddhunter.substack.com/p/reality-is-always-our-friend.
10. Just for fun, here's a list of Bruce Springsteen's most famous work songs: https://www.app.com/story/entertainment/music/2018/09/02/bruce-springsteen-labor-day-boss-7-best-work-songs/1180979002/.

CHAPTER 8

1. Cate Alspaugh, "Art Talk with Makoto Fujimura," National Endowment for the Arts, August 9, 2016, accessed February 16, 2023, https://www.arts.gov/stories/blog/2016/art-talk-makoto-fujimura.
2. "The Carousel Circuit," Visit Binghamton, July 13, 2022, https://visitbinghamton.org/articles/bing-stories/the-carousel-circuit/.
3. "The Formation of IBM: Bundy Time Recording Company (3:43)," Your Audio Tour, accessed February 16, 2023, https://www.youraudiotour.com/tours/315/stops/1326.
4. I'm thankful to theologian W. David O. Taylor for helping me to clarify this section and for sharing this language with me.
5. *Nicene Creed*, Anglican Communion, n.d., accessed February 17, 2023, https://www.anglicancommunion.org/media/109020/Nicene-Creed.pdf.
6. N. T. Wright, *Surprised by Hope: Rethinking Heaven, the Resurrection, and the Mission of the Church* (New York: HarperCollins, 2008), 267.

7. Thanks again to theologian and my friend W. David O. Taylor for this language in *Glimpses of the New Creation: Worship and the Formative Power of the Arts* (Grand Rapids, MI: Eerdmans, 2019).

8. I'm grateful for Tish Harrison Warren's writing on this topic in *Prayer in the Night* (Westmont, IL: InterVarsity Press), 76.

9. I'm grateful to Andy Crouch for deeply influencing my understanding of our God-given roles with culture as creators and cultivators in *Culture Making: Recovering Our Creative Calling* (Downers Grove, IL: InterVarsity Press, 2013).

10. Bishop Todd Hunter, quoted in the Center for Formation, Justice and Peace, "Nourish" series, Day 21 "Peace," https://view.flodesk.com/emails/623c7fac261fb95c1 b089ad1.

CHAPTER 9

1. Dorothy C. Bass, *Receiving the Day: Christian Practices for Opening the Gift of Time* (Minneapolis, MN: Fortress Press, 2019), 58.

2. Later I found the source of the statement from James Bryan Smith, quoted on "228: The Good and Beautiful You with James Bryan Smith—Emily P. Freeman," accessed February 17, 2023, https://emilypfreeman.com/wp-content/uploads/2022/05/The-Next-Right-Thing-Ep.-228.pdf.

3. Adele Ahlberg Calhoun, *Spiritual Disciplines Handbook: Practices That Transform Us* (Westmont, IL: InterVarsity Press, 2015), 42–45.

4. Father Bill Walker, "Labor Day Rest [Christ Church of Austin]," September 2, 2022.

5. "Daily Life," American Institute of Stress, March 30, 2022, https://www.stress.org/daily-life.

6. Juhohn Lee, "Why American Wages Haven't Grown Despite Increases in Productivity," CNBC, July 19, 2022, https://www.cnbc.com/2022/07/19/heres-how-labor-dynamism-affects-wage-growth-in-america.html.

7. Thanks to Bill Walker of Christ Church of Austin for these statistics, which I quote from *CliffNotes* of September 2, 2022, https://christchurchofaustin.org/labor-day-rest/.

8. "38% Of U.S. Pastors Have Thought about Quitting Full-Time Ministry in the Past Year," Barna Group, November 16, 2021, accessed February 19, 2023, https://www.barna.com/research/pastors-well-being/.

9. Kyle Rohane, "Our Pulpits Are Full of Empty Preachers," Christianity Today, April 19, 2022, https://www.christianitytoday.com/ct/2022/may-june/great-resignation-pulpits-full-of-empty-preachers.html.

10. Bobby Gross, *Living the Christian Year: Time to Inhabit the Story of God* (Westmont, IL: InterVarsity Press, 2012), 301.

11. Abraham Joshua Heschel, *The Sabbath: Its Meaning for Modern Man* (New York: Farrar, Straus and Giroux, 1995), 29.

12. Heschel, The Sabbath, 89.

13. The Classical Labyrinth, accessed February 19, 2023, http://www.lessons4living.com/classical.htm#:~:text=Seven%20circuits%20refers%20the%20seven,was%20found%20on%20Cretan%20coins.

14. Eugene H. Peterson, *Working the Angles: The Shape of Pastoral Integrity* (Grand Rapids, MI: William B. Eerdmans Publishing Company, 1987), 68.

15. Tish Harrison Warren, *Liturgy of the Ordinary: Sacred Practices in Everyday Life* (Westmont, IL: InterVarsity Press, 2016), 150.

CHAPTER 10

1. Annie Dillard, *Teaching a Stone to Talk: Expeditions and Encounters* (New York: HarperCollins, 2009), 15.

2. "Viking Cruises Anniversary Sale TV Spot, 'Time'," iSpot.tv | Realtime TV Advertising Performance Measurement, accessed February 19, 2023, https://www.ispot.tv/ad/oWMh/viking-cruises-anniversary-sale-time.

3. Pete Seeger et al., "Turn, Turn, Turn," *Second Hand Songs—A Cover Songs Database*, accessed February 19, 2023, https://secondhandsongs.com/work/40/versions#nav-entity.

4. "Why Native Americans Named the Moons," *The Eastern Trail*, September 13, 2019, https://www.easterntrail.org/why-native-americans-named-the-moons/.

5. George Johnson (not verified) et al., "Harvest Moon: Full Moon in September 2022," *Almanac.com*, September 1, 2022, https://www.almanac.com/content/full-moon-september.

6. Muhammad Adeel Rishi et al., Journal of Clinical Sleep Medicine, "Daylight Saving Time: An American Academy of Sleep Medicine Position Statement," October 15, 2020, accessed February 19, 2023, https://jcsm.aasm.org/doi/10.5664/jcsm.8780.

7. Sandee LaMotte, "Permanent Daylight Saving Time Will Hurt Our Health, Experts Say," CNN, November 6, 2022, https://www.cnn.com/2022/11/06/health/permanent-daylight-savings-health-harms-wellness/index.html.

8. Katherine May, *Wintering: The Power of Rest and Retreat in Difficult Times* (London: Penguin Publishing Group, 2020), 75.

9. May, *Wintering*, 14.

10. May, *Wintering*, 239.

11. Parker J. Palmer, *Let Your Life Speak: Listening for the Voice of Vocation* (San Francisco: Wiley, 2000), 96.

12. Brennan Manning, *Ruthless Trust: The Ragamuffin's Path to God* (New York: HarperCollins, 2010).

13. W. David O. Taylor, "An Advent Calendar: Alternate Narrative, Subversive Time," *Diary of an Arts Pastor*, November 26, 2012, http://artspastor.blogspot.com/2012/11/an-advent-calendar-alternate-narrative.html.

14. Taylor, "An Advent Calendar."

15. Taylor, "An Advent Calendar."

16. Taylor, "An Advent Calendar."

17. N. T. Wright, *On Earth as in Heaven: Daily Wisdom for Twenty-First Century Christians* (New York: HarperCollins, 2022).

18. Wright, *On Earth as in Heaven*.

19. Wright, *On Earth as in Heaven*.

20. Amanda McGill, "Why the Church Year?," *The Homely Hours*, November 23, 2015, https://thehomelyhours.com/2015/10/25/why-the-church-year-2/.

21. Here's a beautiful and meditative description of why the church calendar is illustrated as a circle: Lindsay Bradford-Ewart, *Godly Play Story: "The Circle of the Church Year,"* Godly Play Foundation, accessed February 20, 2023, https://youtu.be/JPTWq1AsCao.

CHAPTER 11

1. Tish Harrison Warren, *Liturgy of the Ordinary: Sacred Practices in Everyday Life* (Westmont, IL: InterVarsity Press, 2016), 24.
2. Scott Russell Sanders, *Staying Put: Making a Home in a Restless World* (Boston: Beacon Press, 1993), 120.
3. *Book of Common Prayer Chapel Edition: Red Hardcover* (New York: Church Publishing, Incorporated, 1979), 392.
4. I've collected community stories about neighbors and neighborhoods here in this series on my website: "Walking Epiphany," https://www.tamarahillmurphy.com/blogthissacramentallife/category/Epiphany.
5. Dallas Willard, *Renovation of the Heart: Putting On the Character of Christ* (Colorado Springs, CO: NavPress, 2014).
6. Brian and I are deeply grateful to NAMI CT for all of the learning and support we received in "Family to Family Fall 2022" class. Statistic quoted in Diagnostic and Statistical Manual of Mental Disorders, 5th Ed. (DSM-5), American Psychiatric Association.
7. DSM-5, 271–272.
8. "I have no peace, no quietness; I have no rest, but only turmoil" (Job 3:26).
9. "I can't lift my soul to God—no light or inspiration enters my soul . . . Heaven, what emptiness—not a single thought of Heaven enters my mind—for there is no hope . . . The place of God in my soul is blank."—Mother Teresa. Brian Kolodiejchuk, *Mother Teresa: Come Be My Light: The Private Writings of the Saint of Calcutta* (London: Crown Publishing Group, 2007), 2.
10. I'm grateful to countless authors and Christians for shepherding my love of reading. The phrase "read outside your tradition" comes from my friend W. David O. Taylor, who I think first heard it from Eugene Peterson.
11. "The Chartres Labyrinth," *Pray With Jill At Chartres*, accessed February 19, 2023, https://praywithjillatchartres.com/labyrinth-2/.

RESPONSE TO PART 3

1. Bishop Todd Hunter, "Reality Is Always Our Friend," *The Gospel of the Kingdom*, December 28, 2022, https://bishoptoddhunter.substack.com/p/reality-is-always-our-friend.
2. Adele Ahlberg Calhoun, *Spiritual Disciplines Handbook: Practices That Transform Us* (Westmont, IL: InterVarsity Press, 2015), 284–6.
3. Calhoun, *Spiritual Disciplines Handbook*, 42–45.
4. Calhoun, *Spiritual Disciplines Handbook*, 42–45.

PART 4

1. "The Chartres Labyrinth," https://praywithjillatchartres.com/labyrinth-2/.

CHAPTER 12

1. Nancy G. Hill, "Tuesday's Top 10 Guest Post: Top 10 When Company's Coming," *Tamara Hill Murphy*, October 13, 2010, https://www.tamarahillmurphy.com/blogthissacramentallife//2010/10/tuesdays-top-10-guest-post-top-10-when.html?rq=company%27s+coming.

2. Leena Oh, "Binghamton Shootings," Homeland Security Digital Library, August 25, 2022, https://www.hsdl.org/c/tl/binghamton-shootings/.

3. Christine D. Pohl, *Making Room: Recovering Hospitality as a Christian Tradition* (Grand Rapids, MI: Eerdmans Publishing Company, 1999), 129.

4. "Chapter 53: The Reception of Guests," Benedictine Abbey of Christ in the Desert, accessed February 19, 2023, https://christdesert.org/rule-of-st-benedict/chapter-53-the-reception-of-guests/.

CHAPTER 13

1. Soong-Chan Rah, *Prophetic Lament: A Call for Justice in Troubled Times* (Westmont, IL: InterVarsity Press, 2015), 73.

2. Latasha Morrison, *Be the Bridge: Pursuing God's Heart for Racial Reconciliation* (New York: Crown Publishing Group, 2019), 41.

3. Fleming Rutledge, *The Crucifixion: Understanding the Death of Jesus Christ* (Grand Rapids, MI: Eerdmans, 2017), 45.

4. Vernée Wilkinson and Tamara Hill Murphy, "Spiritual Practices for Living as an Antiracist Person," *Tamara Hill Murphy*, 2020, https://www.tamarahillmurphy.com/spiritual-practices-for-living-as-an-antiracist-person.

5. I'm forever grateful for each of the writers in this series. They have become a community of fellow sufferers in "Lament Stories," *Tamara Hill Murphy*, accessed February 23, 2023, https://www.tamarahillmurphy.com/lament-stories-2.

6. We're grateful, especially, to W. David O. Taylor for his work in teaching the psalms of lament in W. David O. Taylor, *Open and Unafraid: The Psalms as a Guide to Life* (Nashville, TN: Thomas Nelson, 2020).

CHAPTER 14

1. Eugene C. Kennedy, *The Choice to Be Human: Jesus Alive in the Gospel of Matthew* (Garden City, NY: Doubleday, 1985), 27–28.

2. Marilyn McEntyre, *Speaking Peace in a Climate of Conflict* (Grand Rapids, MI: Eerdmans, 2020), 95–107.

3. This symposium was turned into a wonderful book edited by W. David O. Taylor, *For the Beauty of the Church: Casting a Vision for the Arts* (Ada, MI: Baker Publishing Group, 2010). You can read Eugene Peterson's stories in chapter 4, "The Pastor: How Artists Shape Pastoral Identity."

4. "Session 2: Study Guide," *Conversatio Divina*, January 22, 2022, https://conversatio.org/session-2-study-guide/.

RESPONSE TO PART 4

1. Natalie Jo Evangeline Murphy, "She Writes," Tamara Hill Murphy May 15, 2012, https://www.tamarahillmurphy.com/blogthissacramentallife//2012/05/she-writes.html

2. Vernée Wilkinson and Ted Wueste, "An Examen: Living as an Antiracist Person," *Desert Direction*, February 21, 2021, https://desertdirection.com/2020/06/14/an-examen-living-as-an-antiracist-person/.

3. Ruth Haley Barton, "Martin Luther King Jr. and the Soul of Leadership," Transforming Center, *Beyond Words*, January 13, 2017, transformingcenter.org/2017/01/martin-luther-king-jr-and-the-soul-of-leadership, quoted in Barbara L. Peacock, *Soul Care in African American Practice* (Downers Grove, IL: InterVarsity Press, 2020), 42.

EPILOGUE

1. Angela Wisdom and Susan P. Currie, "Longing to Live in a Spacious Place," Silencio, Issue No. 41, Leadership Transformations, Inc., October 27, 2022.

2. G. K. Chesterton, *Orthodoxy* (Mineola, NY: Dover Publications, 2012), 52.

3. I'm compelled here by Meghan O'Gieblyn's excellent essay "Routine Maintenance," Harper's Magazine, December 20, 2021, https://harpers.org/archive/2022/01/routine-maintenance-embracing-habit-in-an-automated-world-meghan-ogieblyn/.

4. Guy Davenport and Norman Wirzba. *The Art of the Commonplace: The Agrarian Essays of Wendell Berry* (New York: Counterpoint, 2003), 12.

5. Mark R. Day, "Aboriginal Pathways and Trading Routes Were California's First Highways," ICTNews, September 13, 2018, https://ictnews.org/archive/aboriginal-pathways-and-trading-routes-were-californias-first-highways.

6. Margaret Feinberg, "The Difference Taking a Path Versus a Road Makes in Spiritual Growth," *Margaret Feinberg*, accessed February 19, 2023, https://margaretfeinberg.com/margarets-monday-musings-paths-roads-in-lifes-journey/.

7. Thanks to my friend Shannon Coelho for giving us a redemptive vision for navigating Austin's roadways in Shannon Coelho, "Traffic," in *Ordinary Saints: Living Everyday Life to the Glory of God* (Baltimore, MD: Square Halo Books, Inc., 2023), p. 121.

8. Unfortunately, the transcript for this sermon preached at the Sung Eucharist service on Sunday, August 7, 2022, doesn't seem to be available on the Westminster website. You can see Father Bob's biography page here: https://www.westminster-abbey.org/abbey-biographies/the-reverend-robert-latham#i33907.

9. I borrowed these terms from John Mark Comer's helpful sermon about practicing a Rule of Life. John Mark Comer, "Developing a Rule of Life," Bridgetown Church, November 3, 2019, https://bridgetown.church/teachings/unhurrying-with-a-rule-of-life/developing-a-rule-of-life/.

10. Joan Chittister, *In God's Holy Light: Wisdom from the Desert Monastics* (Cincinnati, OH: Franciscan Media, 2013), 132–135 quoted in "Living the Interruptions: Exploring a Rule of Life for 2021." Conversatio Divina, January 22, 2022. https://conversatio.org/living-the-interruptions-exploring-a-rule-of-life-for-2021/.

11. Chittister, *In God's Holy Light*, 132–135, quoted in "Living the Interruptions: Exploring a Rule of Life for 2021," *Conversatio Divina*, January 22, 2022, https://conversatio.org/living-the-interruptions-exploring-a-rule-of-life-for-2021/.

12. See wonderful examples here: https://ruleoflife.com/.

13. Dorothy Day, *The Reckless Way of Love: Notes on Following Jesus* (Walden, NY: Plough Publishing House, 2017).

14. My paraphrase.

15. Wisdom and Currie, "Longing to Live in a Spacious Place."

THE AUTHOR

Tamara Hill Murphy is a spiritual director who has written for publication since 2011 and for a personal website since 2006. Her writing has appeared in *Plough*, *Think Christian*, and the *Englewood Review of Books*. She has worked in ministry roles for twenty-five years and parented four children for over thirty years. She is Supervising Faculty of Selah-Anglican, a Certificate Program in Spiritual Direction with Leadership Transformations, Inc., and a lay leader within the Anglican Church of North America.